Intermediate 2

Computing

Leckie×Leckie

© Scottish Qualifications Authority
All rights reserved. Copying prohibited. No part of this publication may be reproduced, stored in a retrieval system, or transmitted in any form or by any means, electronic, mechanical, photocopying, recording or otherwise.

First exam published in 2004.
Published by Leckie & Leckie Ltd, 3rd Floor, 4 Queen Street, Edinburgh EH2 1JE
tel: 0131 220 6831 fax: 0131 225 9987 enquiries@leckieandleckie.co.uk www.leckieandleckie.co.uk

ISBN 978-1-84372-658-6

A CIP Catalogue record for this book is available from the British Library.

Leckie & Leckie is a division of Huveaux plc.

Leckie & Leckie is grateful to the copyright holders, as credited at the back of the book, for permission to use their material.
Every effort has been made to trace the copyright holders and to obtain their permission for the use of copyright material.
Leckie & Leckie will gladly receive information enabling them to rectify any error or omission in subsequent editions.

[BLANK PAGE]

X017/201

NATIONAL
QUALIFICATIONS
2004

MONDAY, 31 MAY
1.00 PM – 2.30 PM

COMPUTING
INTERMEDIATE 2

Read each question carefully.

Attempt **all** questions in Section I and Section II.

Write your answers in the answer book provided. **Do not** write on the question paper.

Write as neatly as possible.

Answer in sentences wherever possible.

SECTION I

Marks

Attempt ALL questions in this section.

1. An acting agency has created a *multimedia* database. It holds information on actors, such as previous work and pay. It also stores short film clips that can be sent to employers across the world.

   (*a*) What is meant by the term "multimedia"? 1

   (*b*) Suggest an input device that could be used to capture the film clip. 1

   (*c*) Once the film clip has been captured it must be saved on a backing store. It will then be edited to produce a film clip lasting five minutes.

   (i) Suggest a suitable backing store for the film clip. 1

   (ii) Explain why you chose this backing store. 1

   (iii) Access to data on a backing store can be either *serial* or *random*. Explain the difference between "serial" and "random" access. 2

   (*d*) What **type** of application software would be required to send an actor's information electronically to an employer in Australia? 1

   (7)

2. Justin has opened an account with LCL, a new on-line bank. Customers can access their accounts 24 hours a day from a computer linked to the Internet.

   (*a*) Justin downloads his bank statements from his on-line account onto his home computer.

   Suggest a suitable **type** of application software that he could use to **manipulate** the downloaded information on his home computer. 1

   (*b*) When Justin logged on to the on-line bank he was wrongly given access to another customer's account.

   (i) Name the piece of legislation that requires companies to safeguard information held on customers. 1

   (ii) Which stage of the software development process should have detected this problem of unauthorised access? 1

   (*c*) The bank's programmers are working to correct the security problem. Which stage of the software development process are they carrying out? 1

   (4)

Marks

3. Vikram is a trainee programmer who has been asked to write his first program.

   (*a*) He has been advised to implement the program using a high level language.

   Give **two** reasons why he has been advised to use a high level language rather than a low level language. **2**

   (*b*) Name a high level language normally used in:

       (i)   Artificial intelligence **1**

       (ii)   Science. **1**

   (*c*) As part of the software development process, Vikram must design the program.

   Name and describe **one** design methodology. **2**

   (*d*) *Modularity* is a desirable feature of a computer program. Explain why "modularity" would aid the maintainability of a program. **1**

   (*e*) The program's *correctness* must be checked as part of the evaluation stage. What is meant by "correctness"? **1**

   (8)

4. When a computer system is switched on it starts up a program held in ROM.

   This program loads the operating system into RAM.

   (*a*) What is the difference between ROM and RAM? **1**

   (*b*) How does the processor locate where data is stored in memory? **1**

   (*c*) Text, numbers and graphics can be stored in a computer.

   How is **all** data stored in main memory? **1**

   (*d*) State **two** functions of an operating system. **2**

   (*e*) The operating system is part of the *systems software*.

   Name one other type of "systems software". **1**

   (6)

   [Turn over

Marks

5. Jack owns a newsagent's shop which delivers hundreds of newspapers each day. Information about each delivery is stored on Jack's computer.

(*a*) Below is an example of the information stored about a customer.

Initial:	W.A.
Surname:	Stewart
House No:	17
Street:	Rose Terrace
Town:	Johnstown
Newspapers:	Daily Gazette, The Reporter
Papergirl/boy:	Gareth

(i) Suggest the most appropriate **type** of application software to store the customer details.   **1**

(ii) Zoe, a papergirl, requires a list of the addresses on her paper round. Explain how Jack could use the application software to do this.   **3**

(iii) Jack would like a list of all the customers in alphabetical order. Explain how Jack could use the application software to do this.   **2**

(*b*) The shop has a terminal from which Lottery tickets are issued. The terminal uses *machine-readable input*.

Name and describe **one** method of "machine-readable input".   **2**

    (8)

Marks

6. JDLSoftware company is creating a new game.

(a) *Implementation* is one stage of the software development process.

Describe what is done during the "implementation" stage. **1**

(b) Programmers make use of *pre-defined functions*.

(i) What is meant by a "pre-defined function"? **1**

(ii) Give **one** advantage to JDLSoftware of using "pre-defined functions". **1**

(c) In computer games the user interface is one of the most important features of a program. Give **two** examples of features that would make the user interface for a game *fit for purpose*. **2**

(d) The programmers have implemented the program. Describe how the programmers could ensure that the games program has been tested fully. **1**

(e) Once the program has been fully tested it is packaged together with documentation. Suggest **one** item of documentation in the package. **1**

(7)

[END OF SECTION I]

[Turn over for Section II

SECTION II

Attempt ALL questions in this section.

Marks

7. Fiona works in a travel agency and uses a desktop computer. All the computers are linked to a central computer at head office.

   (*a*) Two advantages of having the computers linked together in this way are *data integrity* and *resource sharing*.

       (i) How can the travel agency ensure "data integrity"?   **1**

       (ii) Explain why "resource sharing" is important.   **1**

   (*b*) Information on the central computer is updated continuously.

       State **three** tasks that the company must carry out to ensure suitable backups.   **3**

   (*c*) Recently the *human computer interface* (HCI) of the computer system was changed from a *command driven interface* to a *graphical user interface (GUI)*.

       (i) Explain what is meant by a "human computer interface".   **1**

       (ii) Give **two** reasons why you think the travel agency decided to change the HCI to a "graphical user interface".   **2**

   (*d*) The travel agency is offering a new service where Fiona will visit customers in their own home. She will connect her portable computer system to their telephone line to check availability and make bookings.

       (i) Suggest a suitable **type** of portable computer system that Fiona could use.   **1**

       (ii) Suggest an input device most suitable for a portable computer system with a graphical user interface.   **1**

       (10)

Marks

8. The local golf club is offering junior memberships to children younger than 16 years of age.

The secretary has created his own program in a high level language which requires the user to enter the name, address and age for each child. The program will issue a membership number only if the details are complete and the age is valid.

(*a*) Two types of variable are used in the program for data storage.

Name these **two** types of variable. **2**

(*b*) Describe how the program could make use of a simple conditional statement to check that the child is under 16. **1**

(*c*) Below are three sets of test data used to test the program.

Test Data 1	Name:	Joe Smith
	Address:	
	Age:	14

Test Data 2	Name:	Carrie Eastman
	Address:	14 High Street, Johnstown
	Age:	Thirteen

Test Data 3	Name:	Joe Smith
	Address:	6 Rose Crescent, Johnstown
	Age:	10

Explain why each set of test data has been chosen. **3**

(*d*) The program allows the user to keep entering information until they type EXIT. What type of repetition has been used in this program? **1**

(*e*) When the secretary was coding the program a number of *syntax errors* were generated by the error reporting facility.

   (i) Give an example of a "syntax error". **1**

   (ii) What facility is used to correct a "syntax error"? **1**

(*f*) Explain why a *translator* is needed to run the program. **1**

(10)

[*END OF SECTION II*]

[*END OF QUESTION PAPER*]

[BLANK PAGE]

[BLANK PAGE]

X017/201

NATIONAL
QUALIFICATIONS
2005

MONDAY, 30 MAY
1.00 PM – 2.30 PM

COMPUTING
INTERMEDIATE 2

Read each question carefully.

Attempt **all** questions in Section I and Section II.

Write your answers in the answer book provided. **Do not** write on the question paper.

Write as neatly as possible.

Answer in sentences wherever possible.

SCOTTISH
QUALIFICATIONS
AUTHORITY

©

SECTION I

Attempt ALL questions in this section.

Marks

1. A computer system can be represented by the diagram below.

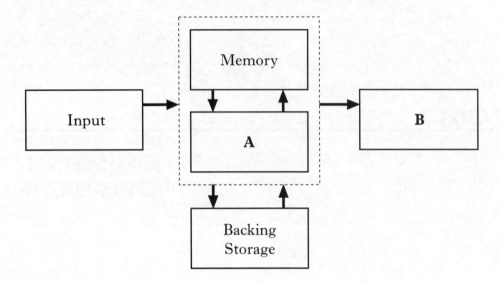

(a) Name the parts **A** and **B**.   2

(b) (i) There are **two** types of memory. What are they called?   2

     (ii) How does a computer know where an item of data is stored in memory?   1

(c) Give an example of **one** magnetic and **one** non-magnetic storage device.   2

         (7)

2. Brendan is a salesman. He is considering buying either a laptop or palmtop computer system. He wants to use his system to show multimedia presentations containing video clips.

(a) Brendan decides to buy a laptop. Using the characteristics of memory and storage, justify Brendan's choice of computer system.   2

(b) Both the laptop and palmtop systems come with an operating system. Describe the following functions of an operating system.

     (i) Memory Management   1

     (ii) File Management   1

         (4)

Marks

3. The music department of Polkirk High School want to produce a computerised presentation of the first year concert.

   (*a*) What type of application would you recommend the music department use to produce their presentation?   **1**

   (*b*) The presentation must include sound. Suggest how the sound could be entered.   **1**

   (*c*) Photographs are input to the computer using a scanner or digital camera. Both devices require an interface.

      (i) Give **two** reasons why an interface would be required.   **2**

      (ii) The camera can take photographs at low resolution, give **one** advantage and **one** disadvantage of the photographs being taken at low resolution.   **2**

      (iii) What type of application would be used to edit the digital photographs?   **1**

   (*d*) A poster is being produced to advertise the concert. The department is considering using a laser or an ink jet printer.

      Give **one** reason for using an ink jet and **one** reason for using a laser printer.   **2**

                                            (9)

[Turn over

Marks

4. A school library system can be accessed using the Internet. This allows pupils to access titles and reviews of books available, both at home and at school.

Below is a diagram of the library system screen.

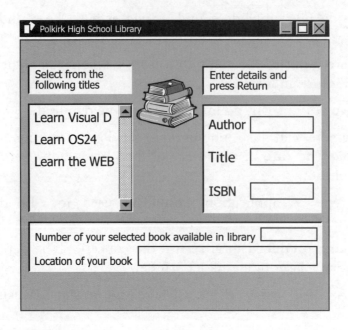

(a) What type of application software would you recommend for storing the library information?

1

(b) What type of application software will the pupils use to access the Internet?

1

(c) Using this library system, what **two** methods could a pupil use to locate a book?

2

(d) Data types are used to store the library information. Suggest **two** data types that the librarian should use to store information on the books.

2

(e) The recording of the borrowing of books is done by scanning a bar code. Explain why either MICR or OCR would be unsuitable for recording the borrowing of books.

1

(f) At the end of the day the librarian makes a backup copy of the library data. Explain the steps involved in making a backup.

2

(9)

Marks

5. A computer program stores the playing card shown below.

(a) What **two** methods could be used to store the graphic in the computer's memory?

2

(b) The playing card could also be represented in text as 7S.

How many bytes would be needed to store this text representation?

1

(3)

6. The software development process consists of 7 stages.

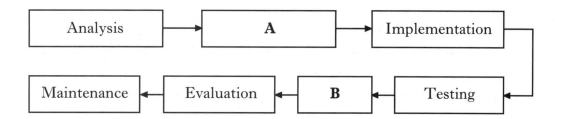

(a) Name the stages **A** and **B**.

2

(b) Describe the purpose of:

(i) the analysis stage;

1

(ii) the evaluation stage.

1

(c) The implementation stage produces a structured listing. What is a structured listing?

1

(d) The software development process is said to be iterative.

What is meant by the term iterative?

1

(e) Solutions to problems can be implemented in procedural or declarative languages.

(i) Name **one** procedural language.

1

(ii) Name **one** declarative language.

1

(8)

[END OF SECTION I]

[Turn over for Section II

SECTION II

Attempt ALL questions in this section.

Marks

7. A local garden centre has asked for software to be written to provide information on various plants they sell. Two types of Human Computer Interface are being considered.

>Find wild blue rose|

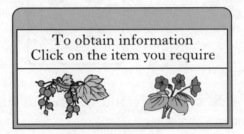

Interface A   Interface B

(a) Name **one** item of documentation that the garden centre should expect to come with the new software application.   1

(b) (i) Explain what is meant by the term Human Computer Interface.   1

    (ii) What type of Human Computer Interface is Interface A?   1

    (iii) What type of Human Computer Interface is Interface B?   1

    (iv) The garden centre decides to use interface B. Give **two** advantages of interface B over interface A.   2

(c) (i) When the software is written, it has to meet the characteristic of "fitness for purpose". What does this mean?   1

    (ii) When the software is written, it has to be documented. Why does the software have to be documented?   1

(d) The garden centre will have networked information points around the store. What **two** advantages are there in using networked systems?   2

(10)

Marks

8. Zoe has used a High Level Language to write a program which uses modularity, control and loop statements.

(*a*) What is modularity and why would Zoe use it? **2**

(*b*) Using a software development environment with which you are familiar, give an example of a control statement. **1**

(*c*) Explain the difference between a conditional and an unconditional loop. **2**

(*d*) The high level language can be translated using a compiler or an interpreter. Explain why Zoe would use:

   (i) a compiler; **1**

   (ii) an interpreter. **1**

(*e*) Zoe enters her code into an *editor*. What is the purpose of an "editor"? **1**

(*f*) One of the programs Zoe is writing needs to ask the user for 2 numbers, add them together and display the result.

Using a design methodology with which you are familiar, design a solution to this problem. **2**

(10)

[END OF SECTION II]

[END OF QUESTION PAPER]

[BLANK PAGE]

Dear Student

In 2005 the format of the Intermediate 2 Computing exam was changed. Two exams were available, one following the format of previous years in this book. This format will not be available in 2006 and beyond.

The following Specimen Question Paper and the actual 2005 exam will give you good practice in the new format. However, the previous years' exams in this book will provide just as good revision and exam-practice features.

Here is some information about the new exam format:

The Question Paper
- contains 3 sections
- is worth up to 70 marks
- is allowed 1 hour 30 minutes.

Section I - 15 marks
- You are expected to attempt all questions in this section, writing short answers.
- The questions test your knowledge and understanding and problem-solving skills in the two mandatory units (Software Development and Computer Systems).
- Approximately 10 marks will be for knowledge and understanding.
- Approximately 5 marks will be for fairly straightforward problem-solving in familiar contexts.

Section II - 30 marks
- You are expected to attempt all questions in this section, writing longer answers that show your structuring and reasoning skills.
- The questions test your knowledge and understanding and problem-solving skills in the two mandatory units (Software Development and Computer Systems).
- Most questions will be subdivided into a number of connected parts with the marks for each part clearly indicated.
- The questions test both knowledge and understanding and problem-solving in less familiar and more complex contexts than those in Section I.
- Approximately 10 marks will be for knowledge and understanding.
- Approximately 20 marks will be for problem-solving.

Section III - 25 marks
- This section has three sub-sections, one for each of the optional units (Artificial Intelligence, Computer Networking and Multimedia Technology).
- You are expected to tackle all the questions within one sub-section, writing longer answers that show your structuring and reasoning skills.
- Most questions will be subdivided into a number of connected parts with the marks for each part clearly indicated.
- The questions test both knowledge and understanding and problem-solving in less familiar and more complex contexts than those in Section I.
- Approximately 8 marks will be for knowledge and understanding.
- Approximately 17 marks will be for problem-solving.
- Some questions, or parts of questions, will need you to use knowledge from the mandatory units.

Please visit *www.sqa.org.uk* for further details.

[BLANK PAGE]

[C206/SQP223]

Computing

Intermediate 2

Specimen Question Paper

Time: 1 hour 30 minutes

NATIONAL QUALIFICATIONS

Attempt Section I and Section II and **one** Part of Section III.

Section I – Attempt all questions.

Section II – Attempt all questions.

Section III– This section has three parts:

        Part A – Artificial Intelligence

        Part B – Computer Networking

        Part C – Multimedia Technology

Choose **one** part and answer **all** of the questions in that part.

Read each question carefully.

Write your answers in the answer book provided. **Do not** write on the question paper.

Write as neatly as possible.

Answer in sentences wherever possible.

SCOTTISH
QUALIFICATIONS
AUTHORITY

©

SECTION I

Attempt ALL questions in this section.

Marks

1. Data is stored in memory using bits.

   What is the largest positive number that can be stored using 4 bits?

   2

2. All computers have an operating system.

   Explain the difference between an operating system and an application program.

   2

3. The design of a program can be represented by *pseudocode*, or by a graphical design notation.

   Name and describe **one** graphical design notation with which you are familiar.

   2

4. Explain why a macro would save time for an application user.

   1

5. Give **one** reason why an interface is needed between a CPU and a peripheral device such as a printer.

   1

6. Software is evaluated in terms of *fitness for purpose, readability* and *user interface*.

   (*a*) Explain the term "fitness for purpose".

   1

   (*b*) Describe how "readability" would help a programmer during the testing stage.

   1

7. Colin finds information about the "Ancient Romans" on the World Wide Web using a search engine.

   What is a search engine?

   1

8. The Arithmetic and Logic Unit (ALU) is part of the processor.

   Name the other **two** parts of the processor.

   2

9. Computer programmers make use of *pre-defined functions*.

   (*a*) What is a "pre-defined function"?

   1

   (*b*) Give **one** example of a standard "pre-defined function".

   1

   (15)

[END OF SECTION I]

SECTION II

Attempt ALL questions in this section.

10. Charles has been asked to create a program that will add up 5 numbers and then display the total. The numbers are typed in by the user and must be in the range 1–100. The design for the program can be represented in pseudocode as follows:

```
1.  take in and add up 5 numbers
2.  show total


Refinement of step 1
1.1  set total to zero
1.2  loop 5 times
1.3      get number from user
1.4      add number to total
1.5  end loop
```

(a) In the design shown above, step 1.2 and step 1.5 represent the beginning and end of a loop.

Name this type of loop.   1

(b) Step 1.3 needs to be further refined. Which **one** of the following standard algorithms would Charles need to use?

- Find minimum
- Count occurrences
- Input validation
- Find maximum
- Linear search   1

(c) After completing the design, Charles used an *editor*.

State **two** features of an "editor".   2

(d) Two of the numbers Charles used to test *normal data* were 17 and 94.

  (i) Suggest **two** numbers Charles should use to test *extreme data*.   1

  (ii) Suggest **two** numbers Charles should use to test *exceptional data*.   1

(e) Charles has poor eyesight. When evaluating his program he found the numbers on the monitor difficult to read.

Describe **two** methods Charles could use to improve the user interface.   2

(f) Charles compiles his program.

Describe how a compiler translates a program into machine code.   1

(g) The program has to be altered to allow the numbers entered to be stored as a list.

What data structure would you use to store the list of numbers?   1

(10)

Marks

11. Below is an advert showing two different types of computer for sale.

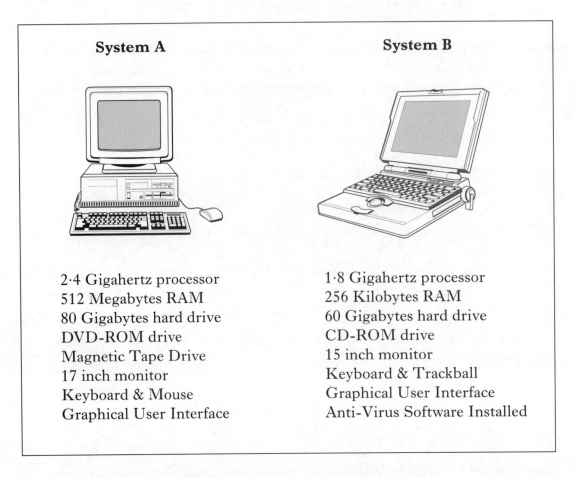

System A

2·4 Gigahertz processor
512 Megabytes RAM
80 Gigabytes hard drive
DVD-ROM drive
Magnetic Tape Drive
17 inch monitor
Keyboard & Mouse
Graphical User Interface

System B

1·8 Gigahertz processor
256 Kilobytes RAM
60 Gigabytes hard drive
CD-ROM drive
15 inch monitor
Keyboard & Trackball
Graphical User Interface
Anti-Virus Software Installed

(a) The advert shown above was created in a graphics package.

From the advert, identify **one** object and **one** operation that may have been carried out on that object. | 2

(b) What is the clock speed of System A? | 1

(c) System A has a DVD-ROM drive, hard drive and magnetic tape drive.

Using **two** suitable characteristics, compare a hard drive with a magnetic tape drive. | 2

(d) System B has anti-virus software.

(i) Describe how a computer virus operates. | 1

(ii) System A has no anti-virus software.

Describe **one** common symptom of computer virus infection. | 1

(e) A technical error has made one of the features of System B unsuitable for a modern computer system.

Identify the technical error and explain your choice. | 2

(f) Explain why a mouse might not be a suitable input device for system B. | 1

(10)

Marks

12. Mrs McNeil's computing class is working on a programming task.

   (a) When writing their programs, pupils often make use of *nested loops* and *logical operators*.

   (i) Explain what is meant by the term "nested loop".   **1**

   (ii) Give **one** example of a "logical operator".   **1**

   (b) The class is writing a program that will calculate the wages of a worker.

   The table below shows the variables used in a program.

Variable Name	Purpose
hours	stores the number of hours worked
rate	stores the hourly rate of pay
wage	stores the wage earned

   The wages are calculated by multiplying the number of hours worked by the hourly rate paid.

   (i) Using a high level language with which you are familiar, write **one** line of code that will calculate how much a worker earns and assign it to the variable wage.   **1**

   (ii) The program calculates the wage of one worker as £314·36.

   Describe how a number like 314·36 is stored in the computer.   **2**

   (iii) When typing the program into the computer, where is the program stored before it is saved to backing storage?   **1**

   (c) The classroom has 20 computers linked in a network.

   (i) Describe **one** economic factor that has led to the development of computer networks.   **1**

   (ii) Mrs McNeil wishes to send the task electronically to a pupil who is ill at home.

   What information does Mrs McNeil need so that she can send the task electronically?   **1**

   (iii) Mrs McNeil has a different type of computer at home from that used in the school. She saved her program in school as both a high level language file and a machine code file.

   Explain why Mrs McNeil was unable to use the machine code file at home but could use the high level language file.   **2**

   (10)

[END OF SECTION II]

SECTION III

Part A—Artificial Intelligence

Marks

Attempt ALL questions in the Artificial Intelligence section.

13. *Eliza* and *chatterbots* simulate conversation between humans and machines.

   (*a*) Give **two** reasons why "Eliza" shows only limited intelligence.   2

   (*b*) Describe **one** commercial application of "chatterbots".   1

   (*c*) Robots that respond to our spoken commands are being developed.

     A busy office introduces a robotic tea trolley that moves around the office and responds to spoken commands like STOP, TEA, COFFEE.

     (i) What area of artificial intelligence is the robot using to understand the commands?   1

     (ii) Suggest **two** factors that may make communication with the robot unreliable.   2

     (iii) The robotic tea trolley is fitted with sensors so that it can move around the office without bumping into the furniture.

      Suggest **two** sensors that would help the robot detect the furniture.   2

     (iv) Give **two** advantages of an *intelligent robot* compared to a robot with no intelligence.   2

                (10)

SECTION III

Marks

Part A—Artificial Intelligence (continued)

14. The Bank of Caledonia has hired a software company to create an *expert system* that can give financial advice. William, the senior financial adviser, has been asked to work with the software company and help create the "expert system".

    (*a*) Suggest **two** reasons why the bank believes it needs an "expert system", rather than relying on human experts.   **2**

    (*b*) Describe William's role during the analysis stage of the development of the "expert system".   **1**

    (*c*) Suggest **one** reason why William may have concerns over the possible use of the "expert system".   **1**

    (*d*) The bank asks the staff in its Stirling branch to use the "expert system" for a trial period.

    Suggest **one** implication for staff using the "expert system" during the trial period.   **1**

    (*e*) "Expert systems" were first developed in the 1970s. Today's "expert systems" hold many more facts and rules.

    State **one** hardware development that has made this possible.   **1**

    (*f*) Give **one** example of an application of an Artificial Neural System that could be used in a bank.   **1**

    (7)

SECTION III

Marks

Part A—Artificial Intelligence (continued)

15. A tourist board has a program written in a declarative language that uses depth first search. The knowledge base holds facts about places in the UK and is used to recommend places to visit.

```
 1  location(blackpool,england). Means Blackpool's location is England
 2  location(caernarvon,wales).
 3  location(edinburgh,scotland).
 4  location(stirling,scotland).
 5  location(linlithgow,scotland).

 6  has(blackpool,tower).        Means Blackpool has a tower
 7  has(caernarvon,castle).
 8  has(edinburgh,castle).
 9  has(stirling,castle).
10  has(linlithgow,palace).

11  american_visit(X) if        Americans will visit X if
    location(X,scotland) and    location of X is Scotland and
    has(X,castle).              X has a castle
```

(a) (i) What would be the result of the following query?

        `location(glasgow,scotland).`   **1**

    (ii) What output will result from the query?

        `has(linlithgow,X).`   **1**

(b) (i) What are **all** the solutions which will be found from the query?

        `american_visit(X).`   **2**

    (ii) Using the numbering system to help you, trace how the system evaluates the query `american_visit(X)` as far as the **first** solution.   **2**

SECTION III

Marks

Part A—Artificial Intelligence (continued)

15. (continued)

(*c*) The diagram below shows a search tree based on a knowledge base of people working in a factory.

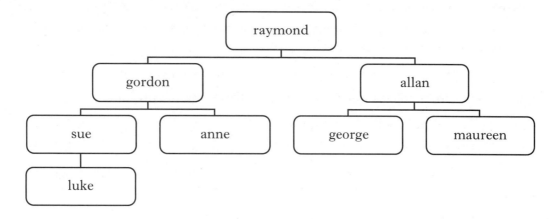

By listing the nodes in the order in which they are visited, describe the search path taken

  (i)   using a breadth first search for allan   **1**

 (ii)   using a depth first search for allan.   **1**

(8)

[END OF SECTION III—PART A—ARTIFICIAL INTELLIGENCE]

SECTION III

Part B—Computer Networking

Marks

Attempt ALL questions in the Computer Networking section.

16. A school library has eight networked computers.

    (a) The library would like to give all eight computers access to the Internet.
    What type of Internet connection would be most suitable for the library?
    Give **one** reason for your answer.   2

    (b) Before using the Internet, library users must agree to a code of conduct.
    Suggest **two** rules that may be contained in this code of conduct.   2

    (c) The library will need an *internet service provider* (ISP).
    Describe the purpose of an ISP.   1

    (d) The library has set up software security measures to stop unauthorised
    access to the Internet.
    Describe **one** example of software security measures.   1

    (e) The library has purchased a Web browser.
    State **two** features you would expect a Web browser to contain.   2

    (f) The following URL was entered:

    http://www.intelligent-games.co.uk

    A few seconds later, the home page of Intelligent Games was displayed on
    the monitor.

       (i) Which service of the Internet is being used?   1

       (ii) What type of software is required to change the URL into an Internet
       Protocol address (IP address)?   1

                                                                              (10)

SECTION III

Marks

Part B—Computer Networking (continued)

17. The QAR bank uses a *leased line* from the public telephone system to transfer customer account details between banks.

(a) Justify why the bank has gone to the expense of using a "leased line".   **1**

(b) Information is transmitted between banks using *asynchronous data transmission*.

     Explain how information is sent using "asynchronous data transmission".   **2**

(c) The bank wishes to intercept and read all messages between banks to ensure the network is being used for authorised purposes only.

    (i) State whether the bank is allowed to intercept and read messages between banks. Give **one** reason for your answer.   **1**

    (ii) Name **one** method of ensuring that the information would be unreadable if it was intercepted.   **1**

(d) A fire has completely destroyed the QAR bank computer and all the data it contained. Within six hours, bank customers were able to access all their account details again.

     How was the bank able to be working again in such a short time?   **2**

         (7)

SECTION III

Marks

Part B—Computer Networking (continued)

18. Roxtel is a small company developing *converging technologies* for the household market.

    (*a*) Explain what is meant by the term "converging technologies"?   **1**

    (*b*) Roxtel intend to create and host a Web page.

    Suggest **two** economic implications for Roxtel of using the Internet for business.   **2**

    (*c*) Each employee has a laptop computer for working at home.

    (i)   The software for the laptop came with a *technical guide*.

    Name **two** contents of a "technical guide".   **2**

    (ii) When an employee takes their laptop into the workplace they do **not** need to attach any cables to access the company network.

    Name **one** piece of hardware that the laptop requires to allow access to the network.   **1**

    (*d*) Data may be transmitted around the network using *unicast, broadcast* or *multicast*.

    What is meant by the term "unicast"?   **1**

    (*e*) One employee used the network to access on-line gambling.

    Describe **one** method of preventing access to this type of website.   **1**

    (8)

[END OF SECTION III—PART B—COMPUTER NETWORKING]

SECTION III

Part C—Multimedia Technology

Marks

Attempt ALL questions in the Multimedia Technology section.

19. Rachel is a singer with a band. She is creating a multimedia website which will allow fans to listen to the band's music, view photographs and read about the band.

    (a) State **two** ways of capturing a photograph of the band.   2

    (b) Once Rachel has the photographs stored on her computer, she decides to edit it to show only a "head and shoulders" photo.

    Name the feature of image editing software that she should use to do this.   1

    (c) Rachel converts the original bit-mapped files into JPEG format.

    What effect will this have on the size of the file?   1

    (d) Rachel records audio clips of the band's music. The software allows her to change the *sampling frequency* and the *sampling depth*.

    ```
    Select settings:

    Sampling frequency        Sampling depth

        ◯   22 kHz                ◯   8 bits
        ◯   44 kHz                ◯   16 bits        [ Continue ]
    ```

    (i) In order to have the best sound quality what settings should she select for *sampling frequency* and *sampling depth*?   1

    (ii) What effect will recording the sound at best quality have on the size of the sound file?   1

    (e) Rachel wants to add *hyperlinks* to her website.

    Describe **two** methods of adding a "hyperlink".   2

    (f) Rachel has completed the implementation stage of creating the website.

    (i) What is the next stage of the development process?   1

    (ii) Describe what Rachel should do at this stage.   1

                                                                                                   (10)

SECTION III

Marks

Part C—Multimedia Technology (continued)

20. Jonathan works for DynamicMedia a company that specialises in the latest technology. They are developing an interactive multimedia presentation to promote the latest *Pocket PC*.

    (*a*) While viewing the presentation, customers are able to listen to audio clips giving reviews and advantages of the "Pocket PCs".

      (i) Name **two** items of hardware that will be needed to **capture** audio.   2

      (ii) Name **two** file types that can be used to store audio.   2

    (*b*) The presentation includes a video clip of people using the "Pocket PC". The video is high quality but the file size is too large. To reduce the file size Jonathan can alter the following properties

    - *colour depth*
    - *resolution*
    - *frame rate*
    - *video time.*

      (i) Select the **two** properties that you think he should change and give a reason to support your recommendation in each case.   2

      (ii) Name **two** items of hardware that a desktop computer will require to display video.   2

    (8)

SECTION III

Marks

Part C—Multimedia Technology (continued)

21. Andrew is creating a multimedia game called Survival. He is using 3-Dimensional (3D) graphics software to create the world where the game is set.

    (a) Andrew defines *textures* for objects. One of the objects he creates is an aeroplane.

    Suggest a suitable "texture" that can be applied to an object like an aeroplane.

    1

    (b) After creating the graphic of an aeroplane, Andrew uses copy and paste to get a second identical aeroplane. He wants it partly hidden behind the first plane. What feature of vector graphics will allow him to do this?

    1

    (c) Andrew creates the 3D world using vector graphics.

    Name **two** file types used to store graphics in vector format.

    2

    (d) Music stored as MIDI files is used in the game.

    Suggest **two** attributes of the sound that could be changed as the game gets more exciting.

    2

    (e) Below is the screen that is shown at the end of the game.

    ```
    TODAY'S TOP SCORER

    ALAN 320 Pts
    ```

    What standard algorithm was used to identify "Today's Top Scorer"?

    1

    (7)

[END OF SECTION III—PART C—MULTIMEDIA TECHNOLOGY]

[END OF SPECIMEN QUESTION PAPER]

[BLANK PAGE]

[BLANK PAGE]

X206/201

NATIONAL
QUALIFICATIONS
2005

MONDAY, 30 MAY
1.00 PM – 2.30 PM

COMPUTING
INTERMEDIATE 2

Attempt Section I and Section II and **one** Part of Section III.

Section I – Attempt all questions.

Section II – Attempt all questions.

Section III – This section has three parts:

   Part A – Artificial Intelligence

   Part B – Computer Networking

   Part C – Multimedia Technology

Choose **one** part and answer **all** of the questions in that part.

Read each question carefully.

Write your answers in the answer book provided. **Do not** write on the question paper.

Write as neatly as possible.

SCOTTISH
QUALIFICATIONS
AUTHORITY

©

SECTION I

Marks

Attempt ALL questions in this section.

1. The *control unit* is one part of the processor.

   Name the other **two** parts of the processor.

2

2. Data is stored in memory using bits.

   What is the largest positive number that can be stored using 7 bits?

2

3. Describe **two** benefits of networking computers rather than having stand-alone computers.

2

4. Mr Williams uses a computer program to record the absences in his class. He types an X beside the name of each absent pupil. At the bottom of the class list, the program shows the total number of pupils absent.

Class 3C2	
Emily Brown	**X**
Jorg Chan-Lau	
Mohammad Hansrod	**X**
Joseph Kelly	
	Absent = **2**

   Which **one** of the following standard algorithms would the program have to use?

   - Find minimum

   - Count occurrences

   - Input validation

   - Find maximum

   - Linear search

1

5. INT and RND are built-in calculations within most High Level Languages.

   What is the correct term for built-in calculations?

1

6. Computer software normally comes with a *technical guide* and a *user guide*.

   Suggest **two** contents you would expect to find in a "user guide".

2

Marks

7. A conditional statement has been designed in pseudocode. It should display the word "teenager" if an age is between 13 and 19 inclusive. The conditional statement is shown below:

    IF age >= 13 OR age <= 19 THEN show the word "teenager"

    When the age 75 is entered the word "teenager" is displayed.

    What mistake has been made in the pseudocode?   1

8. Describe the purpose of a *string variable* in a computer program.   1

9. Describe **one** use of a *text editor* during the software development process.   1

10. Computer viruses have become more common over the last 10 years.

    Describe **two** ways in which computer viruses may be spread.   2

    (15)

[END OF SECTION I]

[Turn over for Section II

Marks

SECTION II

Attempt ALL questions in this section.

11. Mr Richardson is writing a quiz program for his pupils. A choice of answers is given and the user must type the letter (A,B,C or D).

Question: What is the capital of France?

    A   Madrid

    B   Paris

    C   Oslo

    D   Calais

Enter your answer (A,B,C or D): **B**

(a) To make sure that only A,B,C or D is accepted, Mr Richardson includes the following algorithm in the design for his program.

```
1    get answer from keyboard

2    Do while answer < A OR answer > D

3        display error message

4        get answer from keyboard

5    end loop
```

    (i)   Which standard algorithm is Mr Richardson using?   **1**

    (ii)   Explain why this algorithm uses a *conditional loop* rather than a *fixed loop*.   **1**

(b) Mr Richardson codes the algorithm and then tests it.

    (i)   Suggest **one** example of *normal* test data for this algorithm.   **1**

    (ii)   Suggest **one** example of *exceptional* test data for this algorithm.   **1**

(c) Mr Richardson writes his program using a high level language. High level languages can be translated into machine code by an *interpreter* or a *compiler*.

    (i)   Suggest **one** reason why Mr Richardson writes his program in a high level language rather than machine code.   **1**

    (ii)   Describe how a compiler translates programs written in a high level language into machine code.   **1**

    (iii) While he is developing his program, Mr Richardson uses an *interpreter*. Give **one** advantage of using an interpreter rather than a compiler.   **1**

Marks

11. (continued)

(d) Once the pupils have used the program, Mr Richardson decides that the *user interface* could be improved. He wants the user to select the answer from a list, as shown below.

Question: What is the capital of France?

O   Madrid

⦿   Paris

O   Oslo

O   Calais

(i) Which stage of the software development process is Mr Richardson carrying out when he decides that he needs to improve the user interface?   1

(ii) Mr Richardson draws a plan on paper for the new interface.

Which stage of the software development process is being revisited?   1

(iii) Mr Richardson's pupils use laptop computers. Suggest **one** built-in input device that may be used to select the answers.   1

(10)

[Turn over

Marks

12. Fellside High School has produced a magazine to mark its anniversary.

The magazine cover is shown below.

Fellside High School

1905 - 2005
Anniversary Magazine

£3·50

(a) Identify **one** object on the cover and suggest **one** operation that has been carried out on it.   **1**

(b) The articles for the magazine were saved in a standard file format.

   (i) Suggest **one** standard file format suitable for text files.   **1**

   (ii) Explain the advantage of saving the files in a standard format.   **1**

(c) Six pupils sell the magazines at £3·50 each. Janice writes a program that can be used to calculate the money raised.

The design for the program is:

```
1   set total to 0

2   loop from 1 to 6

3      ask pupil for the number of magazines sold

4      add number of magazines sold to the total

5   end loop

6   calculate money raised (multiply total by 3·50)

7   display total and money raised
```

   (i) What design notation has been used above?   **1**

   (ii) In the design shown above, steps 2 and 5 represent the beginning and end of a loop. Name a high level language with which you are familiar, and use this language to write the code for steps 2 and 5.   **2**

   (iii) Janice implements her design by writing code. Suggest **two** ways that Janice can make the code *readable*.   **2**

   (iv) Janice could have calculated the money raised using a spreadsheet. Describe **one** advantage of using a spreadsheet for this task.   **1**

(d) Many former pupils contact the school by e-mail requesting inrformation on events planned for the anniversary year. What feature of e-mail would you recommend to the school so that it can send these former pupils regular information on forthcoming events?   **1**

                                                                             (10)

13. Michelle owns two new computer systems. The specifications for the two systems are shown below.

Marks

SYSTEM A	SYSTEM B
144 MHz processor 16 Mb RAM 8 Mb ROM 3 inch screen (resolution 320 × 320)	2·4 GHz processor 512 Mb RAM 40 GB Hard drive DVD-RW drive 15 inch screen (resolution 1400 × 1050)

(a) Which system described above is a palmtop? Give **one** reason for your answer.

1

(b) System B has a DVD-RW drive. Suggest **one** reason for storing a file on a DVD, rather than the hard drive.

1

(c) System A has a screen *resolution* of 320 × 320.

    (i) Explain what is meant by the term "resolution".

2

    (ii) A black and white image filling the screen, is displayed on system A. Calculate the storage requirements of the image in kilobytes.

    Show all working.

2

(d) Suggest **one** use for ROM on system A.

1

(e) System B can be connected to a printer through an *interface*.

    (i) State **two** functions of an "interface".

2

    (ii) Which type of printer would you recommend for quickly producing fifty high quality copies of a document?

1

(10)

[END OF SECTION II]

[Turn over for Section III

SECTION III

Attempt ONE part of Section III

Choose **one** part and answer **all** of the questions in that part.

Marks

SECTION III

Part A—Artificial Intelligence

Attempt ALL questions in this section.

14. Alan Turing was a computer scientist who helped crack enemy codes during World War II. Today, computers and applications of artificial intelligence are a vital part of military operations. Many computer games have a military theme.

   (a) The *Turing Test* is used to judge the intelligence of a computer system. Describe how the *Turing Test* operates. 2

   (b) State **two** developments in computer hardware that have allowed artificial intelligence applications to become more widely used. 2

   (c) The military use artificial intelligence to study aerial photographs and identify objects. What area of artificial intelligence is being used for this task? 1

   (d) Bomb disposal can be carried out by *intelligent robots*.

   (i) Suggest **one** sensor that would be used by the robot. 1

   (ii) Give **two** reasons for using "intelligent robots" for this task. 2

   (e) Early computer games from the 1950s were very simple compared to today's complex games.

   (i) Name **one** early computer game that demonstrates artificial intelligence. 1

   (ii) Give **one** way in which artificial intelligence has helped to improve computer games. 1

   (10)

15. Techno Travel is a holiday company which has an expert system on its website to help customers find the best route and price for journeys between cities.

   (a) Give **two** advantages to the company of using an expert system, rather than a telephone help-line for this task. 2

   (b) Malcolm obtains information from Techno Travel's website much faster at work than from his home computer. Sometimes he downloads files onto a CD-R that he takes home to load into his own computer.

   (i) Suggest **one** reason why Malcolm can access the website faster at work than at home. 1

   (ii) What precaution should Malcolm take before opening the files from the CD-R on his home computer? 1

   (c) Customers can hire cars on the Techno Travel website. The cars include a speech recognition system which together with route planning software can help travellers find petrol stations, banks and other destinations.

   (i) Suggest **one** task the driver will need to carry out before the speech recognition system can operate effectively. 1

   (ii) Describe **one** problem that could affect the accuracy of the speech recognition system. 1

   (6)

Marks

16. The owner of a double glazing company decides to motivate his staff with rewards like company cars and free holidays. A knowledge base like the one below is used. It contains facts about each employee and rules to decide which reward a member of staff is entitled.

1	`employee(alina,10000).`	*Means Alina is an employee with sales of £10,000*
2	`employee(margaret,29000).`	
3	`employee(jason,10000).`	
4	`employee(tony,26000).`	
5	`manager(alina).`	*Means Alina is a manager*
6	`manager(tony).`	
7	`female(alina).`	*Means Alina is female*
8	`female(margaret).`	
9	`male(jason).`	*Means Jason is male*
10	`male(tony).`	
11	`give_company_car(X) if manager(X).`	*Means give X a company car if X is a manager*
12	`give_free_holiday(X) if employee(X, Y) and Y > 25000.`	*Means give X a free holiday if X is an employee with sales Y and Y is greater than £25000*

(a) What would be the **first** result of the following query?

   `manager(X).`

   1

(b) What would be the result of the following query?

   `female(pauline).`

   1

(c) What would be the result of the following query?

   `give_company_car(margaret).`

   1

(d) What would be **all** the results of the following query?

   `give_free_holiday(X).`

   2

(e) Using the numbering system to help you, trace how the system will evaluate the query

   `give_free_holiday(X).`

   as far as the first solution.

   2

(f) The knowledge base was written in a declarative language that uses *depth first search*.

   Describe what is meant by a "depth first search". You may use a diagram to illustrate your answer.

   2

   (9)

[END OF SECTION III—PART A—ARTIFICIAL INTELLIGENCE]

SECTION III

Marks

Part B—Computer Networking

Attempt ALL questions in this section.

17. Alborough police station is networked through the Internet to national databases. The police use a web browser to access the Internet.

    (a) One of the functions of a web browser is to access the World Wide Web.

    Describe **one** other function of a web browser. 1

    (b) Police have received a message saying that a red car with a registration number starting SN damaged another car and drove off without stopping.

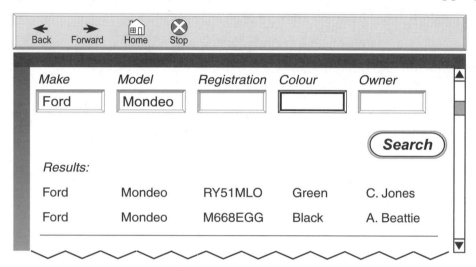

    How could the police use the above screen to identify the owner of the red car? 2

    (c) It is essential that the Internet connection is always available and secure.

    Which type of Internet connection would be most suitable for Alborough police station? 1

    (d) The Internet Protocol (IP) address of the computer in Alborough police station is 129.137.2.56

       (i) Which service allows a name to be used instead of an IP address? 1

       (ii) The URL for the police station may be

    www.alboroughpolice.co.uk

       Explain why this URL would not be suitable for a police station. 1

    (e) Describe **one** physical security measure that could be taken in the police station to stop unauthorised access to national databases. 1

    (f) A prisoner is demanding a printout of his criminal record.

    Explain why the police should not give him a printout of his record. 1

    (g) Alborough police have arrested a trader selling illegal copies of computer games at the local market.

    Which piece of legislation has the trader broken? 1

    (9)

Marks

18. WendyWear is a knitwear company. They have a shop in the Scottish Highlands, but would like to use the Internet to sell their products all over the world.

(a) Describe **two** economic implications of WendyWear creating and hosting a website to sell their knitwear.   2

(b) WendyWear is now selling their products over the Internet.

    (i)   WendyWear are worried about potential threats to the network such as hardware failure.

        Suggest **two** other potential threats to the network.   2

    (ii) Describe a *backup strategy* which would minimise the effect of a hardware failure to the server.   2

    (iii) Enquiries can be e-mailed to WendyWear at

                      enquiries@wendywear.co.uk

        What is the domain name of the above e-mail address?   1

(c) Staff at WendyWear have access to the Internet.

    Give **one** reason why WendyWear may wish to filter access to websites.   1

                                                        (8)

19. Lesley lives in a large house and has a variety of computer hardware including desktop, laptop and palmtop computers.

(a) Lesley is thinking of networking the computers.

    (i)   Give **two** reasons why Lesley would set up a Wireless Local Area Network (WLAN) rather than a Wireless Personal Area Network (WPAN).   2

    (ii) Suggest **two** items of additional hardware which Lesley would need to buy to set up the WLAN.   2

    (iii) Suggest **one** way Lesley could ensure her neighbours would not be able to read the information from her wireless network.   1

(b) Describe **two** differences between the browser Lesley uses on her desktop computer and the microbrowser she uses on her palmtop computer.   2

(c) Lesley used to have a separate games console, DVD player and e-mail facility. She has recently replaced them with a console that does all of these tasks.

    What term is used to describe home appliances with built-in communications capability?   1

                                                          (8)

[END OF SECTION III—PART B—COMPUTER NETWORKING]

SECTION III

Part C—Multimedia Technology

Attempt ALL questions in this section.

20. Pilotville High School has produced a video of their school show.

   (*a*) The video was recorded and transferred to the computer for editing. The video file size was 8·6 gigabytes (Gb).

      (i) To reduce the file size it was compressed using the MPEG format.

        Describe how MPEG compression reduces the file size.   **1**

      (ii) The video file size was still too large. Suggest **two** other ways that the video file size could be reduced.   **2**

      (iii) The video lasted 32 minutes. What feature of the video editing software would allow the video to be reduced to 30 minutes?   **1**

      (iv) The finished video took up 3·8 gigabytes of storage space.

        Suggest a suitable backing storage medium for distributing the video.   **1**

      (v) As each video was copied, it was checked to ensure that it worked correctly on several computers.

        Which step of the software development process is being carried out?   **1**

      (vi) When running the video, the computer kept rebooting unexpectedly.

        Suggest **one** reason for this happening.   **1**

      (vii) On one computer system the sound couldn't be heard. The speakers were tested and found to be working.

        Suggest a piece of hardware that may be faulty or missing from that computer system.   **1**

   (*b*) The front cover of the video will include a picture of the school. Either a digital camera or scanner could be used to input the picture.

      (i) Describe **one** advantage of using a digital camera rather than a scanner to input the picture of the school.   **1**

      (ii) Name **one** piece of hardware found in both a scanner and digital camera.   **1**

          (10)

[Turn over

Marks

21. Digicorp is a company which produces multimedia games for young children.

(a) Digicorp talked to lots of young children to find out what sort of features they would want in their games.

(i) Which stage of the software development process was being carried out?

1

(ii) Many children like 3D images in their games.

One attribute of a vector 3D image is shape. Name **two** other attributes of a vector 3D image.

2

(b) The music to accompany the game will be recorded using a microphone. The recording software allows the *sampling frequency* and the *sampling resolution (sampling depth)* to be altered.

Select settings:

Sampling frequency   Sampling Resolution

   O   44 kHz   O   8 bits

   O   96 kHz   O   16 bits   **Continue**

(i) In order to have the smallest file size, which settings for the "sampling frequency" and "sampling resolution" should be chosen?

2

(ii) Which standard file format for digitised sound would give the best quality sound with the smallest file type?

1

(iii) Instead of recording with a microphone, the music could have been synthesised. Describe **one** method of creating music in this way.

1

(iv) What data format would be used to store the information from the synthesised music?

1

(8)

Marks

22. The logo for a phone company was designed in a vector graphics package. The logo is shown below.

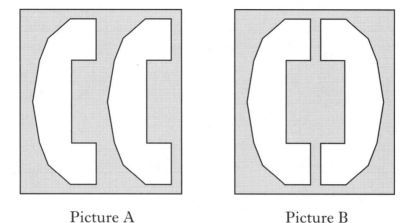

Picture A   Picture B

(*a*) Picture A was drawn then edited to give Picture B.

   (i) Describe how Picture B was created from Picture A.   **1**

   (ii) If the logo is scaled to double its size, what effect would this have on its quality when printed?   **1**

(*b*) What computer hardware is required to display graphics on a monitor?   **1**

(*c*) When first introduced, mobile phones could only be used for making telephone calls.

Describe **two** multimedia features of a *Smart Phone* which were not originally available on mobile phones.   **2**

(*d*) Multimedia applications can run as executable files.

Describe **two** other ways that multimedia applications can be run.   **2**

   (7)

[END OF SECTION III—PART C—MULTIMEDIA TECHNOLOGY]

[END OF QUESTION PAPER]

[BLANK PAGE]

[BLANK PAGE]

X206/201

NATIONAL
QUALIFICATIONS
2006

MONDAY, 29 MAY
1.00 PM – 2.30 PM

COMPUTING
INTERMEDIATE 2

Attempt Section I and Section II and **one** Part of Section III.

Section I – Attempt all questions.

Section II – Attempt all questions.

Section III– This section has three parts:

        Part A – Artificial Intelligence

        Part B – Computer Networking

        Part C – Multimedia Technology

Choose **one** part and answer **all** of the questions in that part.

Read each question carefully.

Write your answers in the answer book provided. **Do not** write on the question paper.

Write as neatly as possible.

Answer in sentences wherever possible.

SCOTTISH
QUALIFICATIONS
AUTHORITY

SECTION I

Attempt ALL questions in this section.

Marks

1. Convert the decimal number 131 to a binary number. **(1)**

2. Explain how real numbers are stored using *floating point representation*. **(2)**

3. The *Control Unit* and the *Arithmetic and Logic Unit* (ALU) are two parts of the processor.

   Name the other part of the processor. **(1)**

4. Many organisations have replaced stand-alone computers with networked computers.

   (a) Describe **one** economic factor that has led to the use of computer networks. **1**

   (b) Describe **one** function of a *server* on a network. **1**

   (2)

5. The text and graphics files for a sixty-four page magazine, containing many large colour photographs, are stored on a hard disk. A copy of the files is to be posted to a commercial printing company.

   (a) Suggest a suitable storage medium for saving the copy of the files that will be sent to the printing company. **1**

   (b) The text files are stored as Rich Text Format (RTF). Suggest a reason for this. **1**

   (2)

6. A pupil uses a high level language to write a program that stores a list of friends' names and mobile phone numbers. When the user enters a friend's name the program finds and displays the friend's mobile number.

   (a) What is the most efficient way to store the list of friends' names? **1**

   (b) Which **one** of the following standard algorithms is the program using to find the friend's details?

   - Input validation
   - Linear search
   - Counting occurrences
   - Find the maximum
   - Find the minimum **1**

   (2)

7. At what stage of the software development process is a *user guide* produced? **(1)**

Marks

8. A program uses a *nested loop* to draw four rows of ten stars on the screen. What is a "nested loop"?

(1)

9. A program written in a high level language must be translated.

    (*a*) Explain why a *translator* is needed.

1

    (*b*) Describe how an *interpreter* operates.

1

(2)

10. Suggest **one** way of improving the *readability* of a program.

(1)

[END OF SECTION I]

[Turn over for Section II

SECTION II

Attempt ALL questions in this section.

Marks

11. Ms Alexander develops a program that will take in the radius of a circle, calculate the area of the circle and display the area of the circle. The radius must be at least 1 cm and not more than 100 cm.

   The main steps of the solution are shown below. Step 3 has been left blank.

1.	Take in radius
2.	Calculate area of circle
3.	

   (a) What is the name of the design notation used above?   **1**

   (b) Step 3 in the design has been left blank. What should Step 3 of the solution be?   **1**

   (c) The algorithm below is used to refine Step 1.

1.1	get number from keyboard
1.2	Do while number <1 OR number >100
1.3	display error message
1.4	get number from keyboard
1.5	end loop

      (i) Describe the purpose of the algorithm shown above.   **1**

     (ii) Steps 1.2 and 1.5 in the algorithm represent a loop. What type of loop do they represent?   **1**

   (d) To calculate the area of a circle, Step 2 is refined as:

2.1	area = 3.14 multiplied by radius squared

      (i) Using a high level language with which you are familiar, write **one** line of program **code** that will calculate the area of the circle.   **2**

     (ii) Some software development environments have a *pre-defined function* to calculate the area of a circle. What is a "pre-defined function"?   **1**

   (e) Ms Alexander tests her finished program using 5 and 27 as examples of *normal* data for the radius. Suggest **two** numbers Ms Alexander should use for *extreme* data.   **2**

   (f) Ms Alexander must evaluate her program in terms of being *fit for purpose*. What does the term "fit for purpose" mean?   **1**

   (10)

Marks

12. Jakub is a businessman who is thinking of buying a computer system for general office work. He has seen the advert shown below.

Standard Features
2·8 Gigahertz processor
1 Gigabyte RAM
2 Megabyte ROM
80 Gigabyte hard drive
CD-R drive
17 inch monitor
300 dpi Colour inkjet printer

Optional upgrades
CD-RW drive
1200 dpi Laser printer

(a) What is the clock speed of the above computer?   1

(b) Main memory is made up of both RAM and ROM.

    (i) Describe **one** difference between RAM and ROM.   1

    (ii) Calculate the total amount of main memory in **megabytes** for the above computer system. Show all working.   2

(c) The advert says that the computer can be upgraded to include a CD-RW drive and laser printer.

    (i) Describe **one** difference between a CD-R and a CD-RW.   1

    (ii) Jakub will be printing off a large number of leaflets advertising his company.

    Describe **two** benefits that Jakub would gain by upgrading to the laser printer.   2

(d) The computer has both operating system software and application software.

    (i) What is the purpose of operating system software?   1

    (ii) The diagram below shows an application program.

	A	B	C	D	E	F
1	City	Leaflets	Orders			
2	Aberdeen	3380	50			
3	Dundee	7839	45			
4	Glasgow	3924	76			
5	Stirling	4516	60			
6	Edinburgh	3035	74			
7						
8						
9						
10						
11						
12						

    From the diagram, identify **one** data object and **one** operation that may have been carried out on that object.   2

    (iii) The chart was created using a *macro*. Describe how the user could record a "macro".   2

(12)

Marks

13. Ramjet Enterprises are using a high level language to write a browser program which includes e-mail facilities.

(*a*) Give **one** reason why they have decided to write the program in a high level language rather than machine code.

1

(*b*) The browser displays *search engine* web pages.

What is a "search engine"?

1

(*c*) The e-mail part of the program allows the user to store a person's nickname, for example George23. What sort of variable would they use to store a person's nickname?

1

(*d*) Before selling the program, Ramjet sends it out to 100 customers to see if it works as expected. The customers will reply by e-mail.

   (i) Which stage of the software development cycle is being carried out?

1

   (ii) Suggest **one** way that all the replies could be collected together in the e-mail software.

1

   (iii) One customer's reply contained a virus.

Describe **two** effects the virus could have upon the computer system.

2

   (iv) If a customer deliberately tried to spread a virus by e-mail, which law would they have been breaking?

1

(8)

[END OF SECTION II]

SECTION III

Attempt ONE part of Section III

Choose **one** part and answer **all** of the questions in that part.

[Turn over

SECTION III
Part A—Artificial Intelligence

Marks

Attempt ALL questions in this section.

14. Many electronic devices and programs on sale today are described as intelligent. Expert systems show their intelligence by storing knowledge and using facts and rules to give advice.

(*a*) Describe **two** abilities which people have that demonstrate human intelligence.

2

(*b*) The *Turing Test* can be used to decide if a computer program is intelligent.

Describe the "Turing Test".

2

(*c*) A printer manufacturer supplies an expert system on CD-ROM with each printer it sells. Customers can solve technical problems with their printer by using the expert system instead of telephoning customer support.

(i) Give **one** advantage to the **customer** of using the expert system rather than the telephone support helpline.

1

(ii) Give **one** advantage to the **printer manufacturer** of using the expert system rather than the telephone support helpline.

1

(*d*) The development of language processing has led to *chatterbots*.

(i) Name an early example of language processing.

1

(ii) Explain why faster processors have led to more effective language processing.

1

(*e*) Future mobile phones may not have a keypad, only an on-off button. Suggest an artificial intelligence application that will allow the user to enter a phone number.

1

(9)

Marks

15. Highland Hideaways is a company that rents out holiday cottages. All the cottages are named after mountains. The knowledge base below shows facts about the cottages and rules for recommending suitable accommodation.

1	has(cairngorm,playarea).
2	has(lomond,garden).
3	has(nevis,playarea).
4	available(cairngorm,july).
5	available(lomond,july).
6	available(lomond,august).
7	available(nevis,september).
8	price(cairngorm,300).
9	price(lomond,200).
10	price(nevis,500).
11	cheap_holiday(X) if
	price(X,Y) and
	Y<250.

(*a*) What would be the result of the following query?

    ?has(cairngorm,garden).   **1**

(*b*) What will be the first solution to the following query?

    ?available(lomond,X).   **1**

(*c*) Below is the start of a trace showing how the system evaluates the query

    ?cheap_holiday(X).

> cheap_holiday(X) matches at 11
>   Subgoal   price (X,Y)
>   matches at 8 X=cairngorm, Y=300
>   Subgoal   Y<250
>   fails

Using the numbering system to help you, complete this trace.   **4**

(*d*) Cottages that are available in July and have play areas are said to be suitable for families and are described as "family choice".

Use this information to complete the following rule:

    family_choice(X)   **2**

[Turn over

Marks

15. (continued)

(e) The search of the holiday cottage knowledge base is carried out by each time expanding the left hand node of the *search tree*, until a solution is found.

Which "search method" is being used?

1

(f) A year later Highland Hideaways buys more cottages to rent and increases the prices of the existing cottages. The knowledge base is updated to include this information.

Which stage of the software development process is being carried out?

1

(10)

16. Malcolm is an estate agent. He visits properties for sale and enters details of the property in his palmtop. He then uses *artificial neural network* software to predict a selling price for the property.

(a)   (i)   What is a "neural network"?

2

    (ii)   Suggest **one** disadvantage of using a "neural network" for this purpose.

1

    (iii)   Malcolm's palmtop has a touch sensitive screen with stylus and no keyboard. Suggest a suitable method of data entry.

1

(b) One of Malcolm's clients is selling a factory building. As part of a safety survey, *intelligent robots* are used to inspect underground water and gas pipes.

Describe how an "intelligent robot" would cope with an obstacle in its path.

2

(6)

[END OF SECTION III—PART A—ARTIFICIAL INTELLIGENCE]

SECTION III

Part B—Computer Networking   *Marks*

Attempt ALL questions in this section.

17. Dr Young works at the Bewell Health Centre. The Health Centre has a *wireless local area network* (WLAN).

    (a) Give **one** advantage for the Health Centre of a WLAN compared to a LAN connected by cables.   **1**

    (b) Dr Young has a laptop computer.

    Name **one** item of hardware that must be installed inside the laptop so that it can connect to the WLAN.   **1**

    (c) The staff in the Health Centre book appointments for patients at the local hospital. A *leased line* connects the Health Centre and the hospital.

        (i) Give **one** advantage of a "leased line" for transmitting data.   **1**

        (ii) Suggest **one** software method of keeping data secure.   **1**

        (iii) Apart from transmitting data to the hospital, suggest **one** other use of the "leased line".   **1**

    (d) Dr Young accesses the World Wide Web for research purposes.

    Describe how he would use a search engine to find out about a drug used in America to treat hay fever.   **2**

    (e) Dr Young sends the following e-mail with a picture of a skin disease to a colleague called Dr Michelle King.

From:	drkenyoung@bewell.nhs.uk
To:	drmichelleking@forth.ac.uk
Subject:	Photo of skin disease

    Attached is a photo showing the current skin problem on the arm of patient X.

    Attached:skinX1.jpg

        (i) Name an input device that could have been used to capture the image.   **1**

        (ii) By looking at Dr King's e-mail address, suggest the type of organisation for which she works.   **1**

    (f) Explain what is meant by *unicast* transmission.   **1**

                                                                                                   (10)

                                                                                        [Turn over

Marks

18. Jamal uses the Internet to buy tickets on-line for musical events. Jamal enters the following URL

http://www.gigs-on-line.co.uk

    (*a*) Which Internet service is Jamal using?   **1**

    (*b*) Once Jamal enters the URL, the Domain Name Service (DNS) carries out *domain name resolution*.

         Describe what happens during "domain name resolution".   **2**

    (*c*) The "gigs-on-line" website uses *data encryption*.

        (i) Suggest **one** reason why they use "data encryption".   **1**

        (ii) The police are investigating ticket sales fraud. They ask to see all encrypted data.

            Which law allows access to data that has been encrypted?   **1**

    (*d*) Jamal enjoys viewing live videos of concerts on the Internet.

         Suggest, with a reason, the most suitable type of Internet connection for this purpose.   **2**

                                                               (7)

19. Derek is responsible for managing the local area network at Hilltop High School.

    (*a*) Give **one** example of a possible physical disaster that could cause the network to fail.   **1**

    (*b*) It is important that data is not lost if the network does fail. Outline an effective backup strategy that will allow the school to recover quickly from data loss.   **2**

    (*c*) Derek has decided that the school should change its Internet Service Provider (ISP) to an ISP that offers a free *filtering* service.

        (i) Explain why it is necessary for the school to use a "filtering" service.   **1**

        (ii) After the filtering software has been in use for a few weeks, Derek decides that the filtering software is not *fit for purpose*.

            Suggest **one** reason for the software not being "fit for purpose".   **1**

        (iii) Apart from a "filtering" service, suggest **one** other service that an ISP normally provides.   **1**

    (*d*) The school has a digital satellite television which features *convergent technology*. The digital satellite television is also connected to the telephone network.

         Suggest **two** ways that this digital television could allow the pupils to become more interactively involved in what they are watching.   **2**

                                                               (8)

[END OF SECTION III—PART B—COMPUTER NETWORKING]

SECTION III

Part C—Multimedia Technology

Marks

Attempt ALL questions in this section.

20. Hamid has been on holiday and taken lots of photographs with his digital camera. He now wishes to create a presentation of his photos to show to his friends.

    (*a*) While he was on holiday, Hamid took 36 photographs that filled up the memory card so that it could hold no more photographs.

       (i) What could Hamid have done **before** he took the photographs, that would have allowed him to store more than 36 photographs on the same memory card? 1

       (ii) **After** he had filled the card, what could he do that would allow him to take more photographs without losing the ones he had already taken? 1

    (*b*) Hamid has imported the pictures into his image-editing program to edit the pictures before he puts them into his presentation.

       (i) Three of the pictures are very dark and difficult to see. What feature of the image-editing software should Hamid use to improve the pictures? 1

       (ii) When the pictures were edited, he had to save the pictures as either GIF or JPEG.

       Describe **two** differences between GIF and JPEG files. 2

    (*c*) Hamid has a choice of using a *WYSIWYG editor* to create a web page or a presentation package to create a presentation.

       (i) What does WYSIWYG stand for? 1

       (ii) What software is needed to view a multimedia web page? 1

    (*d*) Hamid's friends are very impressed and want to take a copy of the presentation home with them.

       (i) The presentation takes up 200 megabytes of disk space. Give **two** reasons why the friends would prefer to have zip disks rather than floppy disks. 2

       (ii) When one of his friends tried the copy at home he was unable to run the presentation. Suggest **one** reason why he was unable to run the presentation. 1

       (10)

[Turn over

Marks

21. Jennifer wishes to send a video message to her relatives in Australia. She records the video then transfers it to the computer to be edited.

   (*a*) In the video editing software, Jennifer reduces the *colour depth* and *video time*.

      (i)   What is meant by the term "colour depth"? **1**

      (ii) What feature of the video editing software would Jennifer use to reduce the "video time"? **1**

      (iii) What effect would reducing the "video time" have upon the video quality? **1**

   (*b*) Jennifer records all the music that she wants to include with the video. Unfortunately, the sound file size is too large. To reduce the file size she uses *lossy compression*.

      (i)   Explain what is meant by the term "lossy compression". **1**

      (ii) Which sound file type uses "lossy compression"? **1**

      (iii) Apart from compression, describe **one** other way the sound file size could have been reduced. **1**

   (*c*) While watching the completed video, Jennifer thinks it is very jerky.

      (i)   What step of the software development process is being carried out? **1**

      (ii) Suggest **one** reason why the video appears jerky. **1**

(8)

Marks

22. Ezetech is hoping to bring *virtual reality* to the home games market with their Ezetech headset.

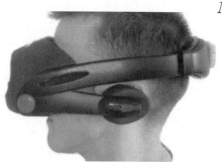

(a) Describe **two** features of multimedia that will have converged in the Ezetech headset.

2

(b) Shown below are two objects from the game.

Object 1   Object 2

(i) Which **two** attributes have been altered between Object 1 and Object 2?

2

(ii) What common file type is likely to have been used to store the graphics for display on the Ezetech headset?

1

(c) The music for their games is created on a MIDI keyboard. The *instrument* is one attribute of a MIDI instruction. Name **two** other attributes of a MIDI instruction.

2

(7)

[END OF SECTION III—PART C—MULTIMEDIA TECHNOLOGY]

[END OF QUESTION PAPER]

[BLANK PAGE]

[BLANK PAGE]

X206/201

NATIONAL
QUALIFICATIONS
2007

MONDAY, 28 MAY
1.00 PM – 2.30 PM

COMPUTING
INTERMEDIATE 2

Attempt Section I and Section II and **one** Part of Section III.

Section I – Attempt all questions.

Section II – Attempt all questions.

Section III – This section has three parts:

> Part A – Artificial Intelligence
>
> Part B – Computer Networking
>
> Part C – Multimedia Technology

Choose **one** part and answer **all** of the questions in that part.

Read each question carefully.

Write your answers in the answer book provided. **Do not** write on the question paper.

Write as neatly as possible.

Answer in sentences wherever possible.

SCOTTISH
QUALIFICATIONS
AUTHORITY
©

SECTION I

Attempt ALL questions in this section.

Marks

1. Three types of computer are listed below:

   desktop, palmtop, mainframe

   (a) Put the three types of computer in order of processing speed, starting with the slowest.

   1

   (b) Name **one** other type of computer **not** listed above.

   1

   (2)

2. Describe **two** benefits of networking computers.

   (2)

3. Floppy disk and hard disk are examples of *magnetic storage media*.

   What type of storage medium is a CD-R?

   (1)

4. A computer processor is made up of three parts.

   Name the part responsible for the temporary storage of data within the processor.

   (1)

5. The Internet is a series of interconnected computers throughout the world.

   (a) Name **one** of the *transmission media* that is used to connect computers on the Internet.

   1

   (b) When using the World Wide Web, a user can type in the web address of a page they wish to look at.

   Suggest **one** other way that a user could go to a web page.

   1

   (2)

6. Jean has compiled a high level language macro into machine code.

   (a) Explain why the machine code program runs faster than the high level language program.

   1

   (b) Jean can run the macro by choosing it from a menu.

   Suggest **one** other way that she would be able to run the macro.

   1

   (2)

7. State the purpose of a *string variable*.

   (1)

8. Using a high level language with which you are familiar, show how you would assign the value 6 to the variable "wage".

   (1)

Marks

9. A programmer is checking to see if a program is *fit for purpose*.

Which stage of the software development process is being carried out? **(1)**

10. The pseudocode shown below uses a *simple condition*.

IF age < 5 THEN display "nursery school"

Create a *complex condition* that will display "primary school" if a person is between the ages of 5 and 11 inclusive. **(2)**

(15)

[END OF SECTION I]

[Turn over for Section II

SECTION II
Attempt ALL questions in this section.

Marks

11. Jenna is a computer programmer. She is trying to decide whether it would be better to upgrade her existing computer or to buy a new computer system.

(*a*) What effect would upgrading the processor have on Jenna's computer? 1

(*b*) Jenna looks at a laptop computer that has an LCD screen.

    (i) What does LCD stand for? 1

    (ii) State **two** reasons why a laptop uses an LCD screen. 2

(*c*) Jenna decides to buy a new computer from her local computer shop. The shop keeps the customer's personal details.

    (i) Name the legislation that allows Jenna to see her personal details. 1

    (ii) Under this legislation, describe **one** right that Jenna has other than seeing her personal information. 1

(*d*) Having bought her new computer, Jenna decides to sell her old computer that she had bought in the year 2005. She has created the following advert to put in the local paper.

```
             FOR SALE
Two year old computer
RAM – 256
Hard Disk – 80
Clock Speed – 2·4 gigahertz (GHz)
```

Jenna has forgotten to put in the units for storage capacity of both RAM and hard disk.

What units should Jenna have used for:

    (i) RAM; 1

    (ii) hard disk? 1

(*e*) Jenna uses a text editor to enter code to create her programs.

    (i) Describe **one** feature of a text editor. 1

    (ii) The documentation that came with the text editor contained a *technical guide*.

    Suggest **one** item of information that should be included in a "technical guide". 1

(10)

Marks

12. The Olympic Games are coming to London in 2012. One of the events will be the 100 metres. A program is being created to control the organisation of the 100 metres.

(*a*) 40 competitors have entered the race. These competitors need to be randomly divided into 5 heats of 8 runners. Part of the algorithm to do this is shown below.

2.1	loop 5 times for heats
2.2	loop 8 times for runners
2.3	pick a random runner
2.4	display runner name, heat number, runner number
2.5	end runners loop
2.6	end heats loop

(i) Both loops use a *fixed loop*.

Describe why a "fixed loop" is used in this situation. 1

(ii) The 'runners loop' is completely contained within the 'heats loop'.

What term is used to describe this situation? 1

(iii) Step 2.3 uses a *pre-defined function* to pick a random runner.

Explain what is meant by the term "pre-defined function". 1

(iv) The 40 names need to be stored.

What data structure would be used to store the 40 names? 1

(*b*) As each competitor crosses the finishing line, a photograph will be taken and their time stored by the computer. The winner will be the first person to cross the line.

(i) Which of the following standard algorithms should the program use to decide the winner?

- Input validation
- Finding the maximum
- Counting occurrences
- Finding the minimum
- Linear search 1

(ii) The photograph is stored as a *bitmap*.

Describe how information is stored in a "bitmap". 1

(iii) Each pixel in the photograph uses 1 bit of memory. The photograph measures 256 pixels across by 80 pixels down.

How much memory in kilobytes will it take to store each photograph? **Show all working**. 2

(iv) Describe **one** advantage of saving the photograph using a *standard file format*. 1

(v) Give **one** reason why hard disk rather than magnetic tape is used as the main backing storage medium. 1

(10)

Marks

13. Rohit is writing a program that will calculate the amount of memory in kilobytes needed to store a square black and white photograph. The length of the photograph must be between 1 and 8 inches inclusive.

The main steps of the solution are shown below.

1.   Take in length of photograph
2.   Calculate memory in kilobytes
3.   Display memory

(a) Show how the above steps would be represented using a *graphical design notation* with which you are familiar. **2**

(b) Input validation is required for Step 1. Using a high level language with which you are familiar, write the **program code** that will take in a number and validate that it is between 1 and 8 inclusive. **3**

(c) Rohit tests his completed program three times using the test data 5, 6, 7. What type of test data is Rohit using in his tests? **1**

(d) When Rohit tries to translate his program, he sees the error messages shown below.

Line 4 – missing "
Line 6 – not found
Line 8 – no END statement

What type of translator is Rohit using? **1**

(e) Rohit fixes all the errors in his code, but before he can save the code, the computer reboots unexpectedly.

   (i) Why might Rohit's computer have rebooted unexpectedly? **1**

   (ii) Suggest a possible solution to this problem. **1**

   (iii) When the computer rebooted, Rohit's program was lost. What part of the computer was storing Rohit's program? **1**

(10)

[END OF SECTION II]

SECTION III

Attempt ONE part of Section III

Part A	**Artificial Intelligence**	**Page 8**	**Questions 14 to 17**
Part B	**Computer Networking**	**Page 12**	**Questions 18 to 20**
Part C	**Multimedia Technology**	**Page 15**	**Questions 21 to 23**

Choose **one** part and answer **all** of the questions in that part.

[Turn over

SECTION III

Part A—Artificial Intelligence

Marks

Attempt ALL questions in this section.

14. Jasmine visits her local computer shop.

   (a) She is interested in the computer advertised below.

   > 8Mb RAM
   > OS v 5.2
   > 320 × 320 colour screen
   > Address book
   > Memo pad
   > Handwriting Recognition Software

   (i) What type of computer is described above?   **1**

   (ii) Describe what Jasmine may need to do when using the handwriting recognition software for the first time.   **2**

   (b) Jasmine buys a computer game where you design your own robot and then send it into battle against other robots controlled by the computer. Each time Jasmine plays, she finds it harder to win.

   (i) What feature should Jasmine include in her robot so that it can detect other robots?   **1**

   (ii) Explain why this game shows more intelligence than early computer games.   **1**

   (iii) Describe **one** use of intelligent robots by the military in real life.   **1**

   (iv) Name the test used to decide if a computer is intelligent.   **1**

       (7)

Marks

15. YesToFinance is a company that specialises in loans, investments and house sales.

(a) YesToFinance uses a software package that learns by being trained with examples. It is then able to predict the answer to similar problems.

    (i) What is this type of system called?   **1**

    (ii) Suggest **one** task for which a finance company could use this type of software.   **1**

(b) YesToFinance also uses a software package called an *expert system*.

    (i) State **two** ways the customer will benefit from an "expert system" being used, rather than a human expert.   **2**

    (ii) Larger hard drive capacity is one example of a development in technology. Explain why this has allowed "expert systems" to be more effective.   **1**

(c) Mrs Harris is buying a flat specially adapted for the elderly. It has a *vision system* which can detect if Mrs Harris has fallen and then alert medical services.

Describe how a "vision system" could detect if Mrs Harris has fallen.   **2**

    (7)

[Turn over

Marks

16. A television company is holding auditions for a talent show. The knowledge base below shows some facts and rules about the competitors.

1 voice(kabira, excellent).
2 voice(sharon, excellent).
3 voice(ryan, fair).
4 voice(jumoke, excellent).
5 dance(kabira, fair).
6 dance(sharon, good).
7 dance(ryan, excellent).
8 dance(jumoke, excellent).

9 is_selected(X) if voice(X, excellent) and dance(X, excellent).
10 is_reserve(X) if voice(X, excellent) and dance(X, good).

(*a*) What would be the result of the following query?

? voice(ryan, fair).

1

(*b*) What would be the first result of the following query?

? dance(X, excellent).

1

(*c*) What would be the result of the following query?

? is_selected(kabira).

1

(*d*) Using the numbering system above to help you, *trace* how the system will evaluate the query

? is_reserve(X).

as far as the first solution.

4

(7)

Marks

17. *Semantic nets* and *search trees* are graphical methods used with knowledge bases. Semantic nets are used to represent knowledge. Search trees illustrate a search through a knowledge base.

(*a*) Draw a semantic net to represent the facts below:

eats(osprey,fish).
is_a(trout,fish).
is_a(salmon,fish).

2

(*b*) A problem is represented using the search tree below.

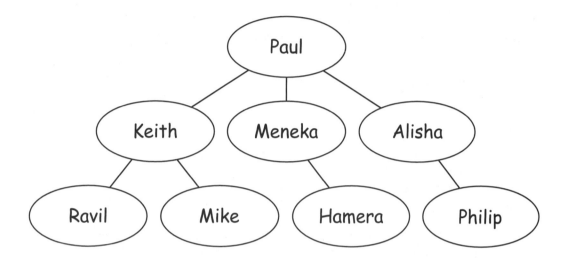

The solution to the problem is Mike.

List which nodes will be visited to reach the solution 'Mike' if the search is:

(i) a *breadth first search*? 1

(ii) a *depth first search*? 1

(4)

[*END OF SECTION III—PART A—ARTIFICIAL INTELLIGENCE*]

SECTION III

Part B—Computer Networking

Marks

Attempt ALL questions in this section.

18. A conference attended by Members of Parliament (MPs) is being held in the Ninian Hotel. Susan is a journalist going to the conference where she will be able to access a wireless LAN and the Internet.

(*a*) What hardware will Susan's laptop need so that it can connect to the wireless LAN?

1

(*b*) Susan logs on to the website for the Ninian Hotel.

Ninian Hotel	
<u>Home</u> <u>Accommodation</u> <u>Restaurant</u> <u>Contact Us</u>	**Availability** Number of rooms [ ] Arrival date [ ] Departure date [ ] **Search**

(i) Susan needs to book one room from 15/08/07 to 17/08/07. Describe how she would check availability using the screen shown above.

2

(ii) The hotel's website has been designed with four *hyperlinks* appearing on every page as shown above. Explain the advantage of using "hyperlinks".

1

(*c*) Susan sends an e-mail to her MP to arrange an interview. Susan's e-mail is shown below.

To:	alistairlennon@forth.gov.uk
From:	susangordon@todaysnews.org.uk
Subject:	

I WOULD LIKE TO INTERVIEW YOU AT THE CONFERENCE. PLEASE CONTACT ME TO ARRANGE A TIME

SUSAN GORDON

(i) Suggest **two** ways that Susan's e-mail may have broken the code of conduct for the use of e-mails at her work.

2

(ii) Susan receives a reply which is *encrypted*. What will Susan need so that she can read the "encrypted" e-mail?

1

(iii) Explain **one** feature of the Regulation of Investigatory Powers Act 2000 that applies to encrypted e-mails.

1

(*d*) At the conference a website explaining e-government is launched.

Describe **one** example of e-government.

1

(9)

Marks

19. Simon enjoys computer games. His favourite game called Granalan has a multiplayer option that allows him to play against other people on the Internet.

(*a*) The game recommends a *broadband* connection to the Internet.

    (i)   Explain what is meant by "broadband".   **1**

    (ii) Suggest **one** reason why a broadband connection would be recommended for the game.   **1**

(*b*) Simon accesses a web page which gives tips on how best to play the game.

The URL is:

http:// <u>www.granalan.com/tips/faq.html</u>

    (i)   What server is hosting this web page?   **1**

    (ii) What is the name of the file being accessed?   **1**

(*c*) The software company that created the game has produced software updates that will fix errors in the program or add extra features to the game. This software is available at the address:

<u>ftp://granalanpatch.com</u>

    (i)   Simon accesses this address and downloads the updates.

        Which Internet service is Simon using?   **1**

    (ii) Simon can log on to the Internet at work, but he is unable to access this address. Suggest a reason for this.   **1**

    (iii) What stage of the software development cycle is being carried out when the company produces these software updates?   **1**

(*d*) Simon has recently installed new e-mail software on his computer. After installing this software, Simon is annoyed to find that his address book is empty.

    (i)   State **one** advantage of an address book.   **1**

    (ii) What should Simon have done to prevent loss of his address book before installing the new software?   **1**

(9)

[Turn over

Marks

20. Mr Harris repairs gas appliances in people's homes. While in the customer's house he forms a network connecting his laptop, PDA and printer. There are no cables connecting the hardware.

(*a*) What type of network is this? 1

(*b*) Due to network failure, Mr Harris has difficulty printing a bill for the customer.

Suggest **one** reason that could cause a network to fail. 1

(*c*) Mr Harris is checking for spare parts on the Internet.

Suggest **one** reason why Mr Harris may prefer to search the World Wide Web using his laptop, rather than using the microbrowser on his WAP phone. 1

(*d*) The software on the laptop allows Mr Harris to create *macros*.

(i) State **one** reason why Mr Harris would recommend using the "macro" feature. 1

(ii) When using the gas company's database, Mr Harris can enter his password and then order parts. Suggest **one** reason why Mr Harris should **not** create a macro for the steps needed to reach the ordering stage. 1

(*e*) Mr Harris tells the customer that *converging technology* can be used when collecting data on gas used and informing the customer of the cost of gas used.

(i) What is meant by "converging technology"? 1

(ii) Suggest how "converging technology" could be used for the processing of gas bills. 1

(7)

[END OF SECTION III—PART B—COMPUTER NETWORKING]

SECTION III

Part C—Multimedia Technology

Attempt ALL questions in this section.

Marks

21. Sophie is creating a multimedia CD.

(a) The sound quality of Sophie's CD will depend on: *sampling resolution* and *sampling frequency*.

Describe what is meant by the term:

   (i) "sampling resolution";   1

   (ii) "sampling frequency".   1

(b) When Sophie's voice is captured with a microphone, the interface must change the signal so it can be used by the computer. What change must be made to the signal?   1

(c) The software used to edit Sophie's voice has a number of editing features.

   (i) Name editing feature A that changed the original sound wave into edited wave 1 as shown below.

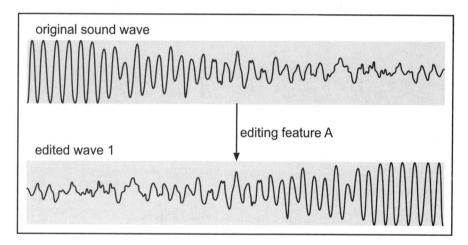

                                                                        1

   (ii) Describe how editing feature B was used to change the original sound wave into edited wave 2 as shown below.

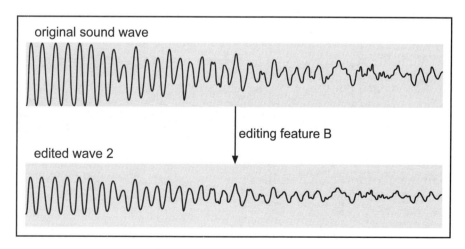

                                                                        1

Marks

21. (continued)

(d) The keyboard track for Sophie's CD has been stored as a MIDI file.

Name **one** attribute of a MIDI instruction. 1

(e) When the CD is inserted into the CD-ROM drive, the following menu appears.

> MENU
>
> Play samples from CD
>
> View Photos
>
> Watch interview with Sophie
>
> *Type Choice:* ▭

Evaluate the multimedia application in terms of difficulties in using the User Interface. 1

(f) The cover for the CD was created in a vector graphics package. After it had been selling for a year, the cover was edited from CD Cover 1 to CD Cover 2, as shown below.

CD Cover 1

CD Cover 2

(i) What feature of a vector graphics package was used to edit CD Cover 1 to CD Cover 2? 1

(ii) What file type is likely to have been used to save CD Cover 1? 1

(iii) The record company wishes to scale the CD cover up to poster size.

Explain why scaling a vector graphic to poster size would not affect printout quality. 1

(iv) If the CD cover had been created using a bit-mapped package instead of a vector graphics package, what effect would this have had on the file size? 1

(11)

Marks

22. Debra has been asked to create a logo for a new gardening show on digital television.

(a) Debra created Logo A using a bitmap graphics package then altered it to Logo B and Logo C.

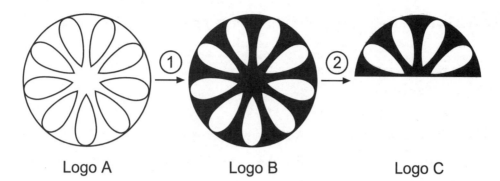

Logo A   Logo B   Logo C

Name the tool that Debra used to alter:

  (i) Logo A into Logo B;   **1**

  (ii) Logo B into Logo C.   **1**

(b) Debra saved two copies of the logo. She saved one copy as a JPEG file and the other as a GIF file.

  (i) State the difference in colour depth between a JPEG file and a GIF file.   **1**

  (ii) JPEG uses *lossy compression*.

       Explain what is meant by the term "lossy compression".   **1**

  (iii) What type of compression does GIF use?   **1**

(c) Debra and the television company use identical monitors. When the logo was displayed on the company's monitor, it did not appear as Debra designed it. Suggest **one** possible hardware reason why the logo does not display as designed.   **1**

(d) Describe **two** tasks that are possible with digital television services that demonstrate the convergence of technology.   **2**

                                                                 (8)

[Turn over

Marks

23. Selicon is a video production company that wishes to put samples of their videos on the company web pages.

(a) Selicon uses a WYSIWYG web page creator when creating the web pages.

Suggest **one** other type of software they could use to create the web pages.　　**1**

(b) Selicon has received a phone call asking what hardware and software are required to view their web pages. They replied:

- A multimedia computer system
- A modem and Internet Service Provider
- Doors 2005 operating system or better.

  (i) Describe the purpose of the operating system software.　　**1**

  (ii) Name **one** type of application software that would be required to view Selicon's web pages.　　**1**

(c) One customer has complained that the videos on the web pages are very jerky when they are played.

In future, how should Selicon alter the settings in the video recording software to ensure the videos are not jerky?　　**1**

(d) As video files take up so much memory, they are compressed using *lossy compression*.

What effect will "lossy compression" have on the video playing time?　　**1**

(e) One of Selicon's employees wishes to make videos at home. She cannot afford a digital video camera.

Suggest **one** other digital hardware device she could use to capture the video.　　**1**

(6)

[END OF SECTION III—PART C—MULTIMEDIA TECHNOLOGY]

[END OF QUESTION PAPER]

[BLANK PAGE]

X206/201

NATIONAL
QUALIFICATIONS
2008

MONDAY, 2 JUNE
9.00 AM – 10.30 AM

COMPUTING
INTERMEDIATE 2

Attempt Section I and Section II and **one** Part of Section III.

Section I – Attempt all questions.

Section II – Attempt all questions.

Section III– This section has three parts:

   Part A – Artificial Intelligence

   Part B – Computer Networking

   Part C – Multimedia Technology

Choose **one** part and answer **all** of the questions in that part.

Read each question carefully.

Write your answers in the answer book provided. **Do not** write on the question paper.

Write as neatly as possible.

Answer in sentences wherever possible.

SECTION I

Attempt ALL questions in this section.

Marks

1. State **two** advantages of using binary numbers rather than decimal numbers in a computer system. **(2)**

2. State **one** function of a *server* on a network. **(1)**

3. A printer is connected to a computer using an *interface*. Describe **one** function of an "interface". **(1)**

4. Describe **one** use of an LCD panel on a printer. **(1)**

5. Describe **one** benefit of using a mailing list when contacting a large number of people by e-mail. **(1)**

6. Sunita can store 75 photographs on a 256 Mb memory card in her digital camera. She alters the settings and can now store 101 photographs on the same memory card. Describe the alteration she has made to the settings. **(1)**

7. Name the stages labelled **X** and **Y** which are missing from the software development process listed below:

   X
   Design
   Y
   Testing
   Documentation
   Evaluation
   Maintenance. **(2)**

8. A teacher evaluates new software and decides it carries out the tasks she wants but the menus and screen layout could be better.

   (*a*) Which **one** of the following has she **not** evaluated:

   - fitness for purpose
   - readability
   - user interface? **1**

   (*b*) Each morning the teacher has to go through a number of steps on the computer to print a list of absent pupils in alphabetical order. Describe what she could do, so that this can be done efficiently in one step. **1**

   (2)

Marks

9. A travel agent wants a program to store an alphabetical list of winter holiday destinations. State the most efficient way to store lists using a programming language.

(1)

10. A conditional statement is used in a program to decide if a discount is given to customers buying theatre tickets.

IF day is Monday OR (age>60 AND day is NOT Saturday) then
    Discount given
ELSE
    No discount
End if

What are the expected results for the following sets of test data?

(*a*)   age = 58, day = Monday **1**

(*b*)   age = 65, day = Saturday **1**

(2)

11. State **one** use for an embedded computer in the home.

(1)

(15)

[END OF SECTION I]

[Turn over for Section II

SECTION II

Attempt ALL questions in this section.

Marks

12. Azam draws the diagram below to represent a computer system.

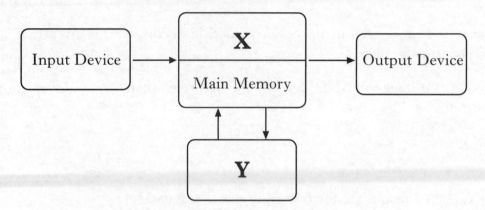

(a) The part labelled **X** contains the *Arithmetic and Logic Unit*, the *Control Unit* and the *Registers*. Name part **X**.

1

(b) Name the part labelled **Y**.

1

(c) Azam visits his local computer shop and notes down the specification of a laptop computer as shown below.

- 2.83 GHz
- 1 Gb RAM
- 512 Mb ROM
- 80 Gb hard drive
- CD-RW drive

(i) What is the *clock speed* of the laptop?

1

(ii) Describe **two** differences, other than cost, between a CD-R disk and a hard disk.

2

(iii) Azam looks at a website that advertises laptops. When he clicks on the words "Laptop Guide" another Web page opens with tips for buying laptops. Explain why this happens.

1

(iv) Name a suitable input device that Azam should buy so that he can use his laptop for video conferencing.

1

(d) Azam designs a program that uses the formula below to convert terabytes to kilobytes.

$$\text{kilobytes} = \text{terabytes multiplied by } 2^{30}$$

Using a high level language with which you are familiar, write the line of **code** for the formula shown above.

2

(e) Azam writes a program in a high level language and it is translated using a compiler. After successfully running the program a few times, he decides to make some changes to it.

Explain why Azam will find it difficult to edit the compiled program.

1

(10)

Marks

13. Roseanne owns a Garden Centre. She has developed a program that asks the user to enter the name and the price of a plant. The program then calculates and displays a table of prices as shown below.

> **Plant**: Geranium
>
> | **Number** | **Cost(£)** |
> |------------|-------------|
> | 1 | 1·50 |
> | 2 | 3·00 |
> | 3 | 4·50 |
> | 4 | 6·00 |
> | 5 | 7·50 |

The design for the program is shown below with step 4 blank:

> 1   get name and price of plant
> 2   display the name of plant
> 3   display the words "Number" and "Cost (£)"
> 4
> 5   display number, number times price
> 6   end loop

(a) What should step 4 of the design be?   **2**

(b) What type of variable should be used to store the name of the plant?   **1**

(c) Pseudocode has been used to represent the design. Name **one** graphical design notation.   **1**

(d) After using the program for several months, Roseanne decides to improve the program by adding a new feature.

Name the stage of the software development process which is being carried out when Roseanne changes her program.   **1**

(e) Roseanne wants the program to check that the price entered in pounds is more than 1 but less than 4. Roseanne refines step 1 as follows:

> 1.1   ask for name of plant
> 1.2   repeat
> 1.3   ask for price of plant
> 1.4   if price <= 1 OR price>=4 then
> 1.5   display error message
> 1.6   end if
> 1.7   until _____

   (i)   Name the standard algorithm being used to check the price.   **1**

  (ii)   Write the condition needed to complete step 1.7   **2**

 (iii)   Once Roseanne has coded the algorithm she tests it with the price £6. Explain why Roseanne used this test data.   **1**

Marks

13. (continued)

(f) Roseanne uses a database to store details of books stocked by the Garden Centre. She uses the database to produce lists of books on special offer.

List A

Title	Price
Bulbs for Spring	£8
Green Lawns	£5
Orchids	£9
Bonsai for Beginners	£3

List B

Title	Price
Orchids	£9
Bulbs for Spring	£8
Green Lawns	£5
Bonsai for Beginners	£3

Identify **one object** and **one operation** that was carried out on that object to change List A into List B.

2

(11)

Marks

14. Harry buys anti-virus software on the Internet. He downloads the software and he also downloads a *user guide* and a *technical guide* for the software.

(a) Name the stage of the software development process at which a "user guide" and a "technical guide" are produced.   1

(b) The format of the files for both guides is *rich text*. Explain why "rich text" is used in this situation.   1

(c) State the type of network to which Harry's computer is connected when he is downloading the software.   1

(d) Harry cannot remember where he saved the file for the user guide. He uses a program which asks him to enter the name of the file and then it finds the file for him.

Which of the following standard algorithms does the program use to find the file:

- Input validation
- Linear search
- Find maximum
- Find minimum
- Count occurrences?   1

(e) Once installed on Harry's computer the anti-virus icon appears on the desktop as a black and white bitmapped graphic. The graphic is 20 pixels by 64 pixels.
Calculate the storage requirements of the icon in bytes.
Show all working.   2

(f) When Harry runs the anti-virus software it detects a virus in the *operating system*.

    (i) State **one** way in which his computer could have been infected by this virus.   1

    (ii) What is the purpose of an "operating system"?   1

(g) Harry gives a copy of the anti-virus software to his brother. Name the law which Harry may have broken.   1

(9)

[END OF SECTION II]

[Turn over for Section III

SECTION III

Attempt ONE part of Section III

Choose **one** part and answer **all** of the questions in that part.

SECTION III

Part A—Artificial Intelligence

Attempt ALL questions in this section.

Marks

15. Newtown Hospital uses *artificial intelligence* applications for some tasks. One example is MedicTalk language processing software. This is installed on the doctors' computers to help communication with foreign patients. The doctor speaks a sentence in English, selects the required language and MedicTalk repeats it in that language.

(a) Describe **one** aspect of human intelligence, other than the ability to communicate.   1

(b) Eliza is an early example of language processing which imitates a conversation with a psychologist.

    (i) Describe **one** reason why it could be argued that Eliza **does not** show intelligence.   1

    (ii) Name the test that can be used to decide if a program is intelligent.   1

    (iii) MedicTalk has a much larger vocabulary than Eliza. Describe **one** hardware development that made this improvement possible.   1

    (iv) MedicTalk uses *speech recognition*. State **one** factor that could affect the accuracy of the "speech recognition".   1

(c) RoboCarrier is an intelligent robot used to deliver medical records within the hospital. If it meets an obstacle it stops and asks the object to move.

    (i) State how RoboCarrier could detect an obstacle in its path.   1

    (ii) As an intelligent robot, describe what RoboCarrier should do if the obstacle does not move.   1

                                                                           (7)

[Turn over

Marks

16. Mr MacDonald is a fruit farmer who is using *artificial intelligence* to improve his crop production. He uses an *expert system* to select the best method of pest control.

(a) Explain what is meant by an "expert system". 1

(b) State **one** advantage of using an "expert system" rather than a human expert. 1

(c) A *vision system* is used to grade apples as perfect or damaged based on their appearance.

Describe how a "vision system" could be used to grade the apples. 2

(d) Mr MacDonald needs a loan from his bank. The bank uses an *artificial neural system* to assess the risk in giving a loan to Mr MacDonald.

   (i) Explain what is meant by an "artificial neural system". 1

   (ii) Describe **one** disadvantage of relying on an "artificial neural system". 1

(e) Mr MacDonald is using the World Wide Web to find dates and locations of Farmers' Markets in Scotland. Describe how he should use the search engine below to obtain this information.

keywords [＿＿＿＿＿＿＿＿] **GoFind!**

2

(8)

17. A travel agent requires a knowledge base about the cost of excursions. A software developer working on this project is creating a *semantic net*.

(a) Name the stage of the software development process which is being carried out. 1

(b) Draw a semantic net to represent the facts below:

Venice is a full day trip
Florence is a full day trip
The price of a full day trip is £32 2

(3)

Marks

18. The solar ultraviolet index (UV index) can be used as a guide to the risk of skin damage from the sun. The knowledge base below shows facts about a UV index forecast for British towns and rules about the level of risk of skin damage.

1 uv_index(blackpool, 2).
2 uv_index(london, 5).
3 uv_index(edinburgh, 3).
4 uv_index(inverness, 4).
5 uv_index(oban, 5).

6 high_risk(X) if uv_index(X,Y) and Y>4.

7 medium_risk(X) if uv_index(X,Y) and Y=4.

8 medium_risk(X) if uv_index(X,Y) and Y=3.

(*a*) What would be the result of the following query:

? uv_index(london, 5).   **1**

(*b*) What would be the **first** solution to:

? medium_risk(X).   **1**

(*c*) Using the numbering system to help you, trace how the system evaluates the query:

? high_risk(oban).   **3**

(*d*) A UV index below 3 is regarded as low risk.

Use this information to complete the following rule:

low_risk(X)   **2**

        (7)

[END OF SECTION III—PART A—ARTIFICIAL INTELLIGENCE]

SECTION III

Part B—Computer Networking

Attempt ALL questions in this section.

Marks

19. Emiko has purchased a laptop computer.

(*a*) When Emiko switches on her laptop, it asks if she wants to connect to a wireless LAN (WLAN). Emiko does not have a WLAN but her neighbour does.

(i) Name the type of transmission that her neighbour's network is using. 1

(ii) Emiko tries to connect to the WLAN. Which part of her neighbour's wireless network hardware is Emiko communicating with? 1

(iii) Emiko was unable to connect to her neighbour's WLAN because of *software security*.

Describe **one** method of implementing "software security". 1

(*b*) Emiko e-mails her friends once a week. She writes her e-mails off-line then connects to the Internet and sends her e-mails.

(i) Explain why Emiko writes her e-mails off-line. 1

(ii) Name the type of Internet connection Emiko is most likely to have. 1

(*c*) Emiko uses a computer at work to send the following e-mail to one of her friends.

To:	charlesyounger@xyz.org
From:	emiko@warmmail.com
Subject:	Video Clip
File(s)	Slipping on a banana.mpg (300Mb)

Hi,

Not sure if you will be interested in this video clip but I thought it was quite funny.

Emiko

(i) Describe how sending this e-mail may have broken the code of conduct concerning the use of Networks and the Internet at her workplace. 1

(ii) By looking at Charles Younger's e-mail address, suggest the type of organisation that he works for. 1

(iii) Name the term used to describe a file that is included as part of an e-mail. 1

(8)

Marks

20. Rachel is a mother of two young children. She works from her home in Livingston and uses the Internet for both business and pleasure. Her two children also use the computer for Internet access.

(*a*) Rachel and her children use a search engine to find information.

```
┌──────────────────────────────────────────────────────────────┐
│                    ┌──────────────────┐  ┌─────────────────┐  │
│   keywords         │                  │  │    Search       │  │
│                    └──────────────────┘  └─────────────────┘  │
└──────────────────────────────────────────────────────────────┘
```

(i) Describe how Rachel would use the search engine to get information on tennis clubs in Livingston. **2**

(ii) Sometimes when the children are using the search engine they get the message "content blocked".

Describe **one** reason why this message appeared. **1**

(iii) Rachel contacts her ISP to find out why some searches have been blocked. What do the letters ISP stand for? **1**

(*b*) Rachel has written an *encryption* computer program which she is going to sell from her website.

(i) Describe the purpose of an "encryption" program. **1**

(ii) The Government has told Rachel that she must give them a copy of the key to her encryption program.

Name the law which states that Rachel should give them a copy of the key. **1**

(iii) Describe **one** economic implication of deciding to sell the program using her website rather than from a shop. **1**

(*c*) One customer has contacted Rachel and asked if he could have a *user guide* for the encryption program. Rachel replied that he can download it from:

http://www.sekrets.com/encrypt/downloads/manual.dok

(i) When the customer enters the URL into his browser, the file is found on the server and downloaded.

Describe how the file is found. **2**

(ii) What is the pathname of the "user guide" in the URL above? **1**

(iii) Describe the purpose of a "user guide". **1**

(*d*) Rachel is concerned that she might lose all the information on her computer, so she copies all her files onto a DVD-RW.

Describe **two** further actions that should be part of Rachel's backup strategy. **2**

(13)

Marks

21. Horst has recently returned home from hospital where he had a heart monitor fitted. This monitor will measure his heart rate and send the information to his palmtop computer.

(*a*) Name the type of communication network described above.

1

(*b*) When the heart monitor is communicating with the palmtop computer, the analogue signal from the monitor must be converted into a digital signal that the computer can understand.

Name the part of the computer that converts the analogue signal into a digital signal.

1

(*c*) If his heart rate gets too high, Horst may need medical treatment.

Describe a suitable use for converging technologies in this situation.

1

(*d*) Horst notices a "signal failure" message on his palmtop.

Name the threat to the network that has occurred.

1

(4)

[END OF SECTION III—PART B—COMPUTER NETWORKING]

SECTION III

Part C—Multimedia Technology

Marks

Attempt ALL questions in this section.

22. Andrew is a photographer who would like to sell his photographs on the World Wide Web.

(a) When Andrew takes a photograph with his digital camera, the light passes through the lens onto the CCD.

Explain the purpose of the CCD in a digital camera.

1

(b) Andrew produces a plan on paper for the Web page that will display his photographs.

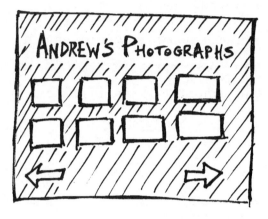

(i) Name the stage of the software development process which Andrew is carrying out.

1

(ii) Each photograph takes up 29360128 bits of memory.

Calculate how many megabytes of memory are equal to 29360128 bits. **Show all working**.

2

(c) Andrew could either use a WYSIWYG editor or a text editor to create his Web page.

(i) Describe how a WYSIWYG editor would be used to create the Web page.

1

(ii) Describe how a text editor would be used to create the Web page.

1

(d) Andrew adds a button saved in GIF format to the Web page. He finds that an outline of the button appears.

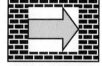

He alters the graphic of the button so that he is able to see through the graphic to the background.

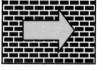

Name the feature of a GIF graphic which allows the background to be seen.

1

(e) Some customers complain that Andrew's Web page is very slow to load over their Internet connection.

Describe **one** alteration Andrew could make to the photographs that would allow faster loading of the Web page.

1

(8)

[Turn over

Marks

23. DigiPhones is developing a video telephone system that allows users to see and hear the person phoning them.

   (*a*) Apart from a digital video camera, name **one** other piece of multimedia input hardware the video telephone system would require.   **1**

   (*b*) DigiPhones is unsure whether to use *synthesised sound data* or *digitised sound data* when capturing the user's voice.

      (i) Explain why "synthesised sound data" would be unsuitable for this purpose.   **1**

      (ii) When digitising sound, one of the factors affecting *sound quality* is the *sampling rate*. Describe the relationship between the "sampling rate" and the "sound quality".   **1**

   (*c*) MP3 files use *lossy compression* to reduce the amount of memory used.

      (i) Describe how "lossy compression" reduces the filesize.   **1**

      (ii) Name **one** uncompressed sound file format.   **1**

   (*d*) When testing the video telephone system, several people complained that the *resolution* of the video was poor.

      (i) Describe what is meant by the term "resolution".   **1**

      (ii) Apart from altering the "resolution", describe **two** ways in which the video quality could be improved.   **2**

   (*e*) DigiPhones would like to create a new ringtone.

      (i) Describe how DigiPhones could **create** the music for a new ringtone and store it on the computer without using a microphone.   **1**

      (ii) The ringtone is tested on the computer and heard through a loudspeaker. Apart from a loudspeaker, what other hardware would be required to output the ringtone?   **1**

   (*f*) Name the correct term used to describe a mobile phone that integrates the functionality of a palmtop computer.   **1**

                                                                     (11)

Marks

24. The image shown below was created using a graphics package.

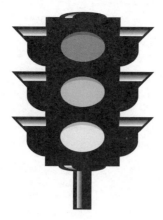

(a) Describe **two** methods you could use to decide if the above graphic was created in a vector graphics package or a bit-mapped graphics package.

2

(b) The graphic was saved using the SVG file type.

State what the letters SVG stand for.

1

(c) Describe how a vector graphic file stores information about each object in the graphic.

1

(d) From the graphic shown above, identify **one** object and **one** operation that may have been carried out on that object.

2

(6)

[END OF SECTION III—PART C—MULTIMEDIA TECHNOLOGY]

[END OF QUESTION PAPER]

[BLANK PAGE]

[BLANK PAGE]

[BLANK PAGE]

[BLANK PAGE]

[BLANK PAGE]